THE LAI

60 ACCESSES TO GREEN RIVER OVERLOOKS

by Jack Bickers

4-WD TRAILGUIDE PUBLICATIONS 1989

Often seen from water level, the magnificent course of this great western river through this deep serpentine gorge is equally astounding when seen from its rims. Over sixty approaches and numerous side-trail attractions are described, depicted and mapped in these pages.

Heading for Entrada Gap (90.3)

**All written material, maps and photographs
are by the author except as noted.**

On Deadman Point at Horseshoe Canyon (57.7)

ISBN: 0-9621507-6-2
Library of Congress Catalog Number: 88-83436

**4-WD TRAILGUIDES PUBLICATIONS
H. B. Jack Bickers
P. O. Box 881
Moab, Utah 84532**

CONTENTS

INTRODUCTION

GENERAL INFORMATION

This is one of the 4-WD Trailguides Publications. Each is a comprehensive guide to trails within a distinct area of the canyon country surrounding Moab, Utah. Each area is defined by a combination of man-made boundaries such as highways and natural barriers such as canyons. Four-wheel-drive is usually necessary to negotiate these trails, however, most of the main roads can be traveled varying distances by two-wheel-drive vehicles.

Where hiking is necessary for visiting a noteworthy feature, the trail is further described as a foot or hiking trail. A vehicular route may be referred to as a "trail" OR a "road." Oftentimes, the USGS mapmakers refer to them as "Jeep Trails." The vast majority of trails are not shown on those maps. This book indicates (in parentheses) the approximate river mile below each rim area approached. Gorge views in either direction vary with severity of bends, but it is possible, with very little hiking, to view nearly every inch of river.

AREAS COVERED BY THIS BOOK

Although this book covers the entire portion of the Green River known as "Labyrinth Canyon", the natural barriers formed by the deep-cut side canyons and the two sides of the river give much division to the overall description of the area.

The first portion begins at the White Wash outlet into the Green, where the river first begins its long, winding entrenchment in an ever-deepening rocky gorge. It ends at Taylor Canyon mouth west of Moab, and is on the Moab side of the river. Between these are Red Wash, Tenmile Canyon, Hey Joe Canyon, Spring Canyon, Hell Roaring Canyon and Mineral Canyon. Each landform is accessible, and has interesting features.

The second portion concerns those points opposite and interlacing those of the first portion. Three Canyon, Bull Hollow, Keg Spring Canyon, Twomile Canyon, Horseshoe Canyon and Deadhorse Canyon are the canyons, and the mesas between them are loaded with intriguing trails and gorgeous rim viewpoints.

A small portion of upper Horseshoe is a separate but equal part of the Maze District of Canyonlands National Park. The northern boundary of Island-in-the-Sky District of Canyonlands follows the north rim of Taylor Canyon, then crosses the Green River. The lower portion of the Green is known as Stillwater Canyon.

Labyrinth Canyon points on the east side are reached from U.S. 191 north from Moab at mile marker 136.7, and also near the 143 mile marker. These are left turns—one onto the Deadhorse Point Road (Utah 313), and the other onto the Blue Hills Road. Points on the west side of the Green are reached from Green

River town, by heading south on the "Green River Road," an Emery
County road which finally joins the main road to Hans Flat
Ranger Station. Contrary to the usual assumption, this dirt
road is very well maintained. This cannot be said of the main
(dirt) roads of the Grand County side.

There are over 60 separate and distinctly different overlook points along the Labyrinth rims—all approachable by 4-WD
vehicles. Very short walks to the rims are usually necessary.
Many good hikes are enumerated here, however, for those who want
to see even more of this astounding country. Bikers and hikers
will find this book will open many exciting new areas to them.

CONTENTS

A comprehensive effort has been made to list and describe
all of the backcountry access roads in the areas covered. Due to
space limitations, some very interesting earlier side trails
leaving the access roads had to be neglected. Where hiking is
required to reach an outstanding viewpoint, some detail is given.
Mileages given must be considered approximate. Most are quite
close. Any destination described has been traveled and checked—
often several times.

It must be remembered that these roads and trails, for the
most part, get little or no maintenance. Cloudbursts can make
big changes in the condition of a road in a few hours—all the
way to a completely impassable washout. In the winter, glazed
dugways are very dangerous. Mid-day snow melts cause mud and
deep ruts which refreeze at night. It is best to let rain-soaked
trails have at least one sunny day in which to dry out.

At this writing, there is no restriction to travel in any
of this BLM-administered country. It is hoped that vehicular
access will always be permitted to this entire beautiful country,
at least for viewing and recreation along the trails.

SUPPLEMENTARY INFORMATION

Guidebooks in the Canyon Country Publications series con-
tain much additional information concerning perimeter roads,
natural history, archeology, camping, hiking, exploration, facil-
ities, services, and jurisdiction.

"Biking, Hiking, and 4-Wheeling Tenmile Canyon," a 4-WD
Trailguides Publication, by Jack Bickers, is an inexpensive guide
to the Tenmile Canyon rims, side canyons and bottom itself.

AREA TERRAIN

Typical high desert country is the description in a nutshell
of this area. The rim of Labyrinth Canyon at its beginning is
only a few feet above water level. Carmel and Entrada buttes are
prominent, and the Navajo Formation is visible. The Wingate makes
its appearance just below Trin Alcove Point's narrow peninsula.
Here, the gorge is about 300 feet deep.

Upriver view from Horseshoe Canyon rim (57.6)

Where Tenmile Canyon enters the Green, by Gary Boynton

Labyrinth's entrenched meander deepens in a few miles, to its maximum of 800 feet at the lower end of Bowknot Bend. Chinle of about 350 feet depth is the base of the Wingate's (usually) vertical walls here, and a thin Kayenta typically separates the Wingate from the Navajo. Exposures of Navajo exist all around, in mesas, rolling hills, domes and deep-cut gullies. The rims hold closely to 4,800 feet elevation, while the river runs at a smooth and steady 4,000 feet.

MAPS

Fifteen-minute quadrangle USGS maps are available in Moab as well as by mail order from the Distribution Center in Denver. They remain the backcountry traveler's greatest aid where maps are concerned. Quadrangles required for Labyrinth Country are: Green River, Crescent Junction, Bowknot Bend, The Knoll, Robbers Roost, The Spur and Upheaval Dome.

A Canyon Country Off-Road Vehicle Trail Map (number 5 of a series), by F. A. Barnes, called "Island Area," is by far the best map available showing all the main access roads on the Grand County side of Labyrinth. Highway turn-off points, Blue Hills Road turn-offs, and even final river-rim destinations of some of the Labyrinth Area trails are shown on this map.

Area maps accompanying their appropriate trail descriptions will be found in this book. These may be best used as a running guide along with the text, as travel progresses. They are shown mainly to illustrate directions of turns and key points.

NAVIGATION

It takes quite a while in the backcountry to acquire the skills necessary in following the old trails. Trails made in seismographing (oil search), sometimes confuse the routes. While there is some valid complaint as to the existence of an excess, many serve as the routes in use today in reaching destinations that may not otherwise be attained.

Unless a trail reaches a definite end—such as a rim, it seldom just ends. The best way to find the continuation of a trail is to get out and walk, assuming that walking is safe. A new trail is never called for. There are plenty, and they reach just about any attainable place anyone could hope to put a vehicle. The trick is to find the trail farther ahead then trace it back to the vehicle. The truly interested visitor will find these trails require a lot of time, and not much will seem to have been accomplished in a day. His curiosity, appreciation of the intricacy of it all, and efforts at better photography, will always take more time than anticipated. This country will not be learned nor seen in a day or two.

Some trails are used frequently at times. Some are used more in certain seasons, and some have not been used for years. It is a fact that some are used when the price of gold is high, but not when it is low. There are times when cattle are brought

in, and times when they are taken out. There are seasons when
trapping is legal, and seasons when it is not. This is typical
of public lands. No oil seems to have been found in the area,
although there is much evidence that seismography and core drilling, as well as test well drilling was done. A quantity of
uranium ore was hauled out of the Bowknot Bend/Spring Canyon/
Hey Joe areas for a time at the turn of the sixties.

Navigation on backcountry vehicle trails is quite enjoyable
in that it sometimes tests the skills of the driver, but more
often his ability to find trail, read maps, and orient himself
with map and visible terrain. Sometimes, a trail segment is
found to be impassable due to deterioration from recent rains.
Learning the general lay of the land by much study of the maps
ahead of time is a great help in going into a new area. It
becomes logical to expect an access in a certain area, and it
will probably be found there.

Newcomers to the canyon country will waste much of their
time if they feel that having four-wheel-drive, they can go where
anyone else can without taking maps and written instructions.
This may be the reason turn-arounds are often seen about half way
out a long trail. After about eight miles of bumping along, he
or his wife says, "I don't see anything out here," and back they
go. What a pity—so near, yet so far! This is what "four-
wheeling" without an objective causes.

Nothing new—except to one's self—will be found in the
destinations of the Labyrinth areas. Word has it that all the
old Indian relics were found long ago. The thrill is in getting
to see this beautiful country. It is still possible to find a
granary—with nothing in it. There are quite a few caves that
still show signs of past habitation. Spring seeps are numerous,
although they may become dry, or nearly so, in late summer.
There are some relatively unpublicized natural arches and bridges
that will absolutely astound the visitors to this country. A
good example is "Natural Arch" on Keg Point at the rim of Twomile Canyon head. It contains five openings—two rooms, two vents
and three front openings.

CAMPING IN LABYRINTH COUNTRY

Where time permits, day trips will allow visits to this wonderful country without camping overnight. This will require an
early start, and a return by dark. The longer days of April
through September will allow the extra time needed merely for
getting out and returning. Venturing far into the backcountry
alone is not advisable. It is better to have another vehicle along
A dependable person should always be given a written plan of
one's projected route, destination, and return time. Camping out
for a night eliminates one round trip, and allows a great benefit
in time saved just traveling.

For a lone traveler, it is even more important that the above
information be left with someone trustworthy. Persons traveling
with no other people or vehicles along are the most vulnerable to

Beautiful bend in Tenmile Canyon bottom

White Wash enters the Green River (93.3)

accident without nearby help. This is especially true in hiking
away from the vehicle. It behooves one to be exceedingly cautious
in rock hiking. A canteen of water, some emergency food and
matches should be carried along when hiking away from the camp
or vehicle, even though a long hike is not anticipated.

There are some hardy souls who camp out for several nights
alone. Even winter does not hamper them too much. This is not a
recommended practice for newcomers to this country. Almost
everyone camping for an extended period will have another vehicle
along, or at least an able companion. It is not a good idea to take
someone along who does not anticipate the campout with enthu-
siasm. Remember, it's not everyone's cup of tea. It is not fun,
in the long run, when one does all the work, while the other remains bored. Let them do their "own thing" elsewhere.

Camping is permitted in these public lands almost anywhere
one finds an acceptable spot. There are certain common-sense re-
strictions. One would certainly not wish to camp where cattle
gather. Their waterholes and trails do not make desirable camping
places.

A river bottom may be used by river rafters at a desirable
sandy beach, but a bottom as usually reached by land vehicles is
not often a good camping spot since cattle may frequent the
beautiful cottonwood groves. Insects such as deer flies and
mosquitoes may be bothersome. Camping in in a dampish, heavily
shaded place is inadvisable since tree spiders, black widows and
snakes may have concentrated there.

The best camping spot is out on the open mesa itself. If
the weather is cool, a place should be found where sunrise will
hit the camp early. If a very warm evening is expected, then a
place shaded by high rock should be chosen. If children are
along, the camp should be located away from dangerous rims so
they will be safer while the adults go about the camping chores.

Bureau of Land Management rules require that all trash be
carried out. Dead and down wood may be gathered, but fires must
be made in safe places. Range fires are devastating and costly,
and those responsible for causing them can be prosecuted.

THE SEASONS OF LABYRINTH

The high desert climate of the Labyrinth areas is just about
the same as Moab's in the lower elevations, and about the same as
Arches National Park in the upper portions. The prime times for
visiting Labyrinth areas are during the months of April and May
in the spring, and September and October in the fall. "Indian
Summer", is the finest of all, and sometimes extends well into
November. March could have a bit of quick-melting snow and will
be somewhat colder, but this is no real problem if one realizes
that summer has not yet arrived—especially at night—and outfits
himself accordingly. November nights are colder than October
nights and are to be so considered when preparing to visit these
areas.

June, July and August—especially July—are the hot months,

and temperatures in mid-afternoon often exceed 100 degrees. The heat is more noticeable when hiking.   It will require more water and shady rest stops.   Hikes should begin early in the morning to finish by noon. With a top on the vehicle, and maximum ventilation, travel is not unbearable even even in mid-afternoon. Mornings are nearly always cool until about 10:30 a. m. and nighttime coolness always sets in at sundown. If summer conditions are properly dealt with, it is most assuredly a very fine season for visiting Labyrinth country.

Most Labyrinth country is in elevations of 4,100 to 4,900 feet. Trails on The Spur will run from 6,000 down to 4,800 feet elevations. It is interesting to note that the latitude of Deadman Point is exactly that of Moab.

Fine vehicle & expert driver on June's trail

Below San Rafael River mouth, from opposite side (93.4)

Where White Wash turns red

Tenmile gorge from "Natural Arch" trail

RIVER MILES AT RIM APPROACHES

MILES	ACCESS	SIDE
95.1	San Rafael River--North side	west
94.4	San Rafael River--South side	west
93.3	Tenmile Point	east
92.7	Bull Bottom	west
92.7	Tenmile Point	east
91.6	Tenmile Point	east
91.4	Bull Bottom	west
90.3	Bull Bottom	west
89.6	Tenmile Point	east
89.0	Tenmile Point	east
88.3	Bull Bottom	west
88.0	Trin Alcove	west
88.0	Tenmile Point	east
87.0	Tenmile Point	east
86.4	Junes Bottom	west
85.2	Junes Bottom	west
85.0	Tenmile Point	east
83.0	Tenmile Point	east
82.2	Tenmile Point	east
80.0	Tenmile Point	east
79.3	Tenmile Bottom Overlook	west
78.6	Tenmile Bottom Overlook	west
78.6	Tenmile Canyon Bottom	east
78.0	Tenmile Bottom Overlook	west
77.3	Tenmile Bottom Overlook	west
77.0	Oil Well Road	east
76.0	Oil Well Road	east
75.1	Hey Joe and the Arches	east
75.0	Oil Well Road	east
74.8	Hey Joe and the Arches	east
74.4	Hey Joe and the Arches	east
74.0	Hey Joe and the Arches	east
73.1	Hey Joe and the Arches	east
72.0	Spring Canyon Point	east
71.0	Keg Point	west
70.4	Keg Point	west
69.0	Spring Canyon Point	east
68.5	Keg Point	west
68.4	Spring Canyon Point	east
66.3	Spring Canyon Point	east
66.0	Deadman Point	east
65.0	Spring Canyon Point	east
64.5	Deadman Point	east
64.0	Deadman Point	east
63.4	Deadman Point	east
62.5	Deadman Point	east

61.4 .....Deadman Point ....east
61.2 .....Keg Point ....west
60.3 .....Deadman Point ....east
59.0 .....Keg Point ....west
58.1 .....Keg Point ....west
57.7 .....The Spur ....west
57.7 .....Deadman Point ....east
56.7 .....The Spur ....west
56.0 .....The Spur ....west
54.0 .....Deadman Point ....east
53.8 .....Mineral Point ....east
52.3 .....Mineral Point ....east
51.1 .....Mineral Point ....east
50.8 .....Mineral Point ....east
50.8 .....Horsethief Point ....east
50.0 .....Horsethief Point ....east
49.0 .....The Spur ....west
43.4 .....Horsethief Point ....east

Bull Bottom upstream trail (92.2)

Although there are some alternate routings available in a few trails, this guidebook will adhere to describing the best and shortest route. In some instances, cross-over trails exist, but are not described and may, or may not, appear in the Segment Maps. No assurance is guaranteed or implied as to the travel-worthiness of any trail. Rains in the past two years prior to publication of this book have harmed trails on this side more than the damage accumulated in 20 years prior. Wet weather times are not good times to use any trail, and glazed (frozen) grades are extremely dangerous. The back country traveler has to rely on his own good judgement and ability. There is no maintenance on the lesser roads, and not enough, if any, on the major ones, especially on this east side.

No gasoline, cold drinks or McD's will be found in this country. Persons traveling backcountry must provide themselves with all needs prior to leaving town. If the vehicle's reliability becomes doubtful, it is time to return to home base.

TENMILE POINT ROAD

This road is accessed by turning left off U.S. 191 (north from Moab) onto the Blue Hills Road near the 143 Mile Marker. At about 5-1/2 miles, the left turn to Dubinkey Well Road (south) will be passed. In another 2 miles, the road crosses two deep dips in Mancos Shale dirt flats. After a few left and right curves (2 more miles), a signed left turn goes up a slight grade southward. This is TENMILE POINT ROAD. It gradually drops while crossing several cross-drains.

After reaching a broad prairie, a major left turn is noticed. This is DRIPPING SPRINGS ROAD. TENMILE POINT ROAD continues southwestward. The next intersection of note is the RUBY RANCH/WHITE WASH ROAD--a right fork. Again, the main trail continues southwestward. Many trails leave this road before it reaches the Green River. These are described under headings of their own.

SPRING CANYON POINT ROAD

Here, the access is via Utah 313, the Deadhorse Point Road. It leaves U.S. 191 north of Moab at about mile 136.7, a left turn. At Mile Marker 14, a BLM sign indicates a right turn onto DUBINKY WELL ROAD. In slightly over a mile, DUBINKY WELL ROAD forks right. In about 6 miles, Dubinky windmill will be seen soon after a cattle guard is crossed. SPRING CANYON POINT ROAD forks left, then, about 250 yards prior to reaching the

windmill.   Some people confuse this POINT road with the
Spring Canyon BOTTOM road--which was the left fork mentioned prior to this.   The Point road has a number of
side-trail attractions that are further described.

SPRING CANYON BOTTOM TRAIL

     Accessed   as in the above POINT trail, except the
left, or straight-away, continuation is taken when the
fork is reached in about 1-1/4 miles after turning onto
Dubinky Well Road.   At this writing, this road remains
suitable for two-wheel-drive, except the dugway into
Spring Canyon has deteriorated considerably.   Expert
Jeepers and motorcycle riders sometimes go down the
dugway.   Otherwise, this road is the key to a myriad of
side roads leading to Green River and side canyon over-
looks--mainly in the DEADMAN POINT area.   These are
further described.

DEADMAN POINT ROAD

     An old cattlemen's route, beginning as a trail off
DUBINKY WELL ROAD about 1/2 mile prior to reaching
Dubinky windmill, and before crossing a cattleguard.   In
its southward run, it crosses SPRING CANYON BOTTOM ROAD.
This crossing about 6 miles out, furnishes the best
access to DEADMAN POINT ROAD.
     Many of the most spectacular points are reached
from the DEADMAN POINT ROAD.   Where time is limited, it
will lead the viewer to more beautiful Labyrinth Canyon
miles of river gorge than any other trail available, and
in a shorter time.   Views of the Bowknot Narrows, Twomile Rim Arch, Horseshoe Canyon mouth, the Horseshoe
Rincon, The Spur, Keg Point, Spring Canyon, Hell Roaring
Canyon, and Bowknot "Island" can all be had from the
Deadman Point rims.

MINERAL POINT ROAD

     This long trail is a right turn from the Dead Horse
Point Road beyond the 11 mile signpost.   Three major
viewpoints of Labyrinth Canyon are available, as well as
views into the North and South Forks of Mineral Canyon
along the south rim, and Hell Roaring Canyon rims along
the north edges.   Many fine trails over the ridge
prominences, shady camping places, and hikes into mountain sheep areas will be found in this area.

HORSETHIEF POINT/MINERAL BOTTOM ROAD

     Only about a quarter-mile beyond the Mineral Point
main turn-off and at a prominent BLM sign, the Horse-
thief/Mineral Bottom road leaves the Dead Horse Point
Road (Utah 313), forking right.   This road is used for
entering the White Rim Trail (Canyonlands National

Old San Rafael River bridge site

The present-day San Rafael River bridge

Park), and for river-rafting activities. In good weather, this road is usually in good condition as it receives somewhat more maintenance than others, due to its importance to these various activities. Several interesting side trails leave this road--some having connections with the Taylor Canyon rim trails, which are not extensively described in this guidebook.

Just prior to its beginning the drop from the mesa to the river bottom, the main trail has an old trail crossing. A right turn on this leads shortly to spectacular Mineral Bottom overlooks. A left turn here leads to Taylor Canyon rim. Hikes along the river gorge rim can be taken, leading back to the main trail. This could entail hiking distances from almost nothing to four or five miles, depending on the amount of hiking one wished to do. A very small corner of Canyonlands National Park is entered here.

BIG DRAW/BEEHIVE BUTTE/WHITBECK ROCK TRAILS

These trails all travel diagonally along the south side of the Horsethief Point ridge prominence to overlooks along Taylor Canyon.

The Whitbeck Rock vehicular trail ends at the Canyonlands National Park boundary. A hike of about 1.5 miles reaches the rim and views of point formations called Moses and Zeus which attract rock climbers.

The Beehive Butte trail is easy enough and furnishes a better, but cross-canyon, view of Moses and Zeus, and can be had without entering Park boundaries or appreciable hiking.

The Big Draw Trail is longer, sandier and more venturesome. It ends at a big natural bridge called Grand Central What? This is a breath-taking overlook of Taylor's wide lower portion and a distant view of Labyrinth Canyon. A hike of about a mile can connect with the hike originating from the Horsethief spur trail described in the HORSETHIEF POINT article.

All three of these trails leave from Utah 313, taking the Island in the Sky branch, then leaving it in right turns 1 and 2 miles beyond the paved intersection at mile 8.

These exciting trails will not be further described since they do not lead to Labyrinth Canyon rim points. This mention may suffice for the avid visitor to this area. The topographic maps show the basic approaches to these trails. The Knoll and Upheaval Dome quadrangles cover this area. The updated Canyonlands National Park Map shows the later boundary changes in this area. Generally, the boundary follows Taylor Canyon rims, but there are two places where they cut across from side inlets, and these are marked.

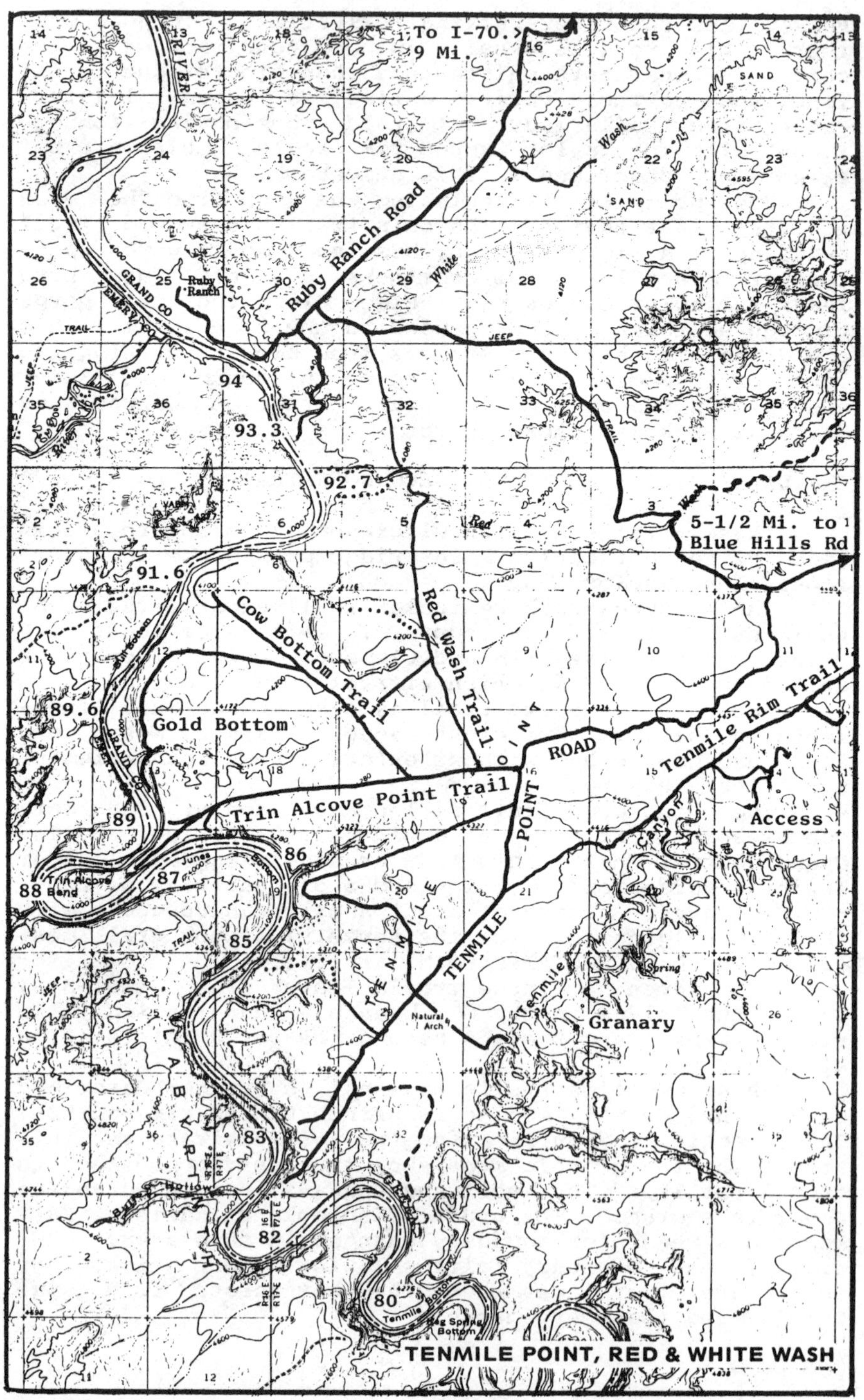

14
13
To I-70.
9 Mi.
16
15
14
13
RIVER
SAND
23
24
19
20
21
Wash
22
23
24
SAND
Ruby Ranch Road
26
GRAND CO.
EMERY CO.
25
Ruby Ranch
30
29
White
28
27
26
25
JEEP
94
TRAIL
35
36
31
32
33
34
35
36
93.3
TRAIL
92.7
2
6
5
Red
4
3
5-1/2 Mi. to
Blue Hills Rd
91.6
6
4
3
Cow Bottom Trail
11
12
Red Wash Trail
9
10
89.6
Gold Bottom
18
ROAD
Tenmile Rim Trail
15
P O I N T
Trin Alcove Point Trail
Canyon
Access
89
Junes
16
15
86
20
21
87
TENMILE
88
Trin Alcove
Bend
85
TENMILE
Tenmile
Spring
Natural
Arch
Granary
26
36
L A B Y R I N T H
83
82
80
Tenmile
Bottom
Big Spring
Bottom
TENMILE POINT, RED & WHITE WASH

Trail Segments - East

TRAIL NAME: T E N M I L E   P O I N T

TYPE: Spur, with many side branches.

MAPS: Crescent Junction and Bowknot Bend Quadrangles.

MILEAGE: 15 miles one way to the Point proper.

TIME: 1.5 hours to the Point, disregarding side trails.

DIFFICULTY: Routine, easy driving with careful attention to bumps and dips. Road condition poor.

ACCESS: A left turn off Blue Hills Road about 10 miles out from U.S. 191 near mile-marker 143.

TRAIL SUMMARY: This main trail furnishes access to TENMILE CANYON BOTTOM, TENMILE WEST RIM trail, DRIPPING SPRINGS ROAD, and WHITE WASH/RUBY RANCH ROAD--in addition to several branches near its end to superb Labyrinth Rim overlooks and river-bottom entries.

TRAIL DESCRIPTION:

The first intersection of note along Tenmile Point Road is the left turn onto the DRIPPING SPRINGS ROAD at about 5-1/2 miles, but in less than a mile, another left turn also heads for Dripping Springs. Beyond the DRIPPING SPRINGS ROAD turns, the WHITE WASH/RUBY RANCH ROAD is next to appear in about 1/2-mile, forking to the right. This connecting road runs westward for about 8 miles, first crossing Red Wash, then White Wash, then meeting the Ruby Ranch Road coming in from I-70.

Red Wash can be driven upstream for 1-1/4 miles. A climb-out onto Entrada tops is nice. A natural rock window and some black rock plugs are interesting.

A right turn at White Wash runs upstream and is a very nice trip. This is a favorite run for motorcycles and ATV's. It is a good place to camp, and the lower rim is accessible in good weather for trailers, provided they enter from the Ruby Ranch Road route from I-70.

A left turn onto Ruby Ranch Road soon reaches a left turn off the road for a short jaunt down the wash. A short hike (250 yards), leads to a nice view of the Green River (93.3). The banks are low and muddy. Driving too far down the wash bottom is hazardous as the soft putty-like silt has a thin cover of sand that may appear to be dry. A beautiful grove of Cottonwoods grows along the opposite bank. The rise of the gorge rims and the Navajo layer begins just downstream. The opposite bank is the upstream portion of BULL BOTTOM, and is easily accessible by vehicle to the water's edge on that side.

Back on the main Tenmile Point Road, and in about

3 miles, the road makes a bend to the left. At the end of a low escarpment on the left, there is a corral which is a good landmark.

Just beyond this bend, a fork leads away in a westerly direction. This easy spur runs about 3-1/2 miles and ends nearly halfway out and atop the Trin Alcove Bend peninsula (88). This is one of the most spectacular accesses of the entire Labyrinth Canyon portion of the Green River Gorge. At this point, the canyon walls have risen to about 300 feet, and just downstream from the lower bend of Trin Alcove Point, the Kayenta layer emerges.

Two short spurs leave the TRIN ALCOVE POINT TRAIL about 1/4 mile from the trail's end. The left spur overlooks the river at the lower bend (87) at the General Land Office section marker 13/18 over 24/19. With binoculars, the old and rough JUNES BOTTOM TRAIL on the opposite side of the river can be readily traced. Can THAT be done? It is discussed in the Western Labyrinth Trails section of this book.

The short spur leaving the Point trail to the right is a bit beyond the aforementioned spur. This gives good upstream views into the Green's gorge (89), and the accessible bottoms mentioned above. It is probably the most spectacular photography point of upper Labyrinth. A rock dropped from the sheer north rim of the Point would nearly fall into the river. It is easy to hike to the Point bottom, but the lower terrace is a thicket. Directly opposite is the mouth of Three Canyon (Trin Alcove), a favorite stopping place for river runners. That side has the advantage of good ingress, afternoon shade and morning sun. It is very beautiful to see Trin Alcove Point from that side's rim.

1/4 mile after leaving the main TENMILE POINT ROAD on this TRIN ALCOVE POINT TRAIL, a fork to the right leads to LOWER RED WASH, reaching it in about 3-1/2 miles. There is an easy way into the wash bottom, but there may be soft places. The wash bottom is very nice, with big trees on grassy banks. The river (92.7) shore can be reached through the wash bottom, but walking is advised as water level varies. An easy trail out northwestward leads to the main White Wash trail just prior to its crossing and reaching Ruby Ranch Road.

A 1/2-mile beyond the above RED WASH TRAIL fork, a second right fork goes into the bottoms land just below a very old section marker; 1/6 over 12/7. This is a nice, shady bottom (91.6) but is used by cattle. Very close to the trail's entry of this bottom, and on the opposite side of the river, is an old stock trail carved down the near-vertical cliff and into BULL BOTTOM. This is readily accessible from that side of the river.

A left fork on this trail less than a mile from its end, goes down the rocks in a very interesting trail to a bottom downstream (89.6), and just above the Trin Alcove bend. At this writing, claims are being held current here, and are not to be molested. Cattle graze this bottom as well, but it is a very interesting four-wheel drive trip giving a feeling of accomplishment both in having made the trip, and in seeing the spectacular gorge views.

Back on the MAIN TRAIL, and shortly another trail departs to the right. In about 2 miles, this trail reaches a rocky rim on the Green that provides one of the best views of Labyrinth (85) at a gorge depth of about 300 feet. This overlook has a rougher alternate return route, but its departure is hard to find.

The MAIN POINT TRAIL veers very shortly to a southwesterly direction. This is the point at which the road is joined by the main TENMILE WEST RIM trail.

In about 1-1/2 miles, the next important junction is reached. This is the Natural Arch Rock junction. This side trail leaves the main trail (left) and heads southeast past this rock, reaching Tenmile Canyon rim in less than a mile. An eye-popping view awaits on a nearby point. The canyon is deeply entrenched in its lower gorge. The Navajo rim sits back roughly, seemingly to give the inner gorge plenty of space to meander as it likes. A study of the very rough, pure rock rims on the opposite side of Tenmile gives the impression of absolute inaccessibility. To the contrary, this is some of the finest point travel in the entire Labyrinth country.

Passing or leaving the Natural Arch Rock turn-off, the main Tenmile Point Road runs about a mile, and an old well site is seen just to the left of the trail. A rough, hard-to-define trail does continue over the rocks and finally reaches the rim (83). However, this is NOT the TRUE extent of the Point trail. Actually, the trail turns left by the old water well site, and heads south up the low rim. This easy trail turns westward to the extreme end of vehicular travel on a narrow, edgy point (82.2). It is one of the grandest viewpoints of the roughest, most sinuous, but not the deepest, portions of Labyrinth Canyon.

Not very far beyond the old water well site, a dim trail runs south (a left turn) for a mile, and overlooks the last tight meander of Tenmile Canyon as it enters the river (80). This is another outstanding view into the rough depths and bends of Labyrinth.

NOTES: This very wide area called Tenmile Point is actually a series of sub-points. This is because several river bends and side canyons have created so many separate points. It will be very hard to decide which would be the best to visit. The view into Tenmile's lower gorge is fabulous. Trin Alcove Point is astounding, and so is the very sharp and narrow Tenmile Point just described (92.2). An early start and close attention to the map will help visitors to enjoy more without having to spend time finding the desired trail. An overnight campout is a grand experience in this area.

Tenmile Canyon mouth seen from "The Very End" (78.8)

Gold Bottom seen from Trin Alcove Point (89.4)

TRAIL NAME: D R I P P I N G   S P R I N G S   R O A D

TYPE: Connecting; with spurs.

MAPS: Crescent Junction and The Knoll quadrangles.

MILEAGE: 1-1/2 miles.

TIME: 15 minutes (See Summary).

DIFFICULTY: Easy, but deep loose sand prior to reaching Tenmile streambed.

ACCESS: This short segment is a left turn off the Tenmile Point main trail about 5-1/2 miles below its origin at the Blue Hills Road junction.

TRAIL SUMMARY: This road reaches the streambed of Tenmile Canyon just upstream of the high-perched Dripping Springs. This route continues out of the canyon, heading southeast. It joins the SPRING CANYON POINT ROAD in about 6-1/4 miles; therefore, that connecting segment will be described in that section. The DRIPPING SPRINGS ROAD segment may be used for reaching either the TENMILE BOTTOM TRAIL or the TENMILE WEST RIM TRAIL. Their departures from this segment are given under their own headings.

TRAIL DESCRIPTION:

The wide left turn onto the Dripping Springs Road from the Tenmile Point main road would be hard to miss, even though a signpost may no longer exist at this point. The first portion is eroded hard-pack, and the latter is deep, loose sand. Views upstream and downstream of Tenmile's exit of Carmel/Entrada rims and entry of Navajo dome country, become very interesting here.
The trail drops abruptly into the streambed. The rock complexes, cottonwood groves, and low, sandy benches are beautiful. Dripping Springs is situated slightly downstream, but rather high on the west rim. A bucket may be noticed hanging at the seep. Poison Ivy may be present.
This trail continues, and climbs out the east rim to make connection with SPRING CANYON POINT ROAD. This 6-1/4 mile portion is described in the SPRING CANYON POINT section.
TENMILE BOTTOM and the EAST and WEST RIM TRAILS are served by this road, and hiking, biking, camping and four-wheeling in this area are exhilerating experiences unmatched elsewhere in the Canyon Country. These trails are described following this.

TRAIL NAME: T E N M I L E   W E S T   R I M

TYPE: Connecting; with spurs.

MAPS: The Knoll and Bowknot Bend quadrangles.

MILEAGE: About 6 miles.

TIME: 1-1/2 hours if little time is spent enjoying the
rim points. An entire day could be spent here.

DIFFICULTY: Easy. Short stretches of sand.

ACCESS: Easiest access by leaving the main TENMILE
POINT ROAD at the DRIPPING SPRINGS ROAD (a left turn).
Just prior to reaching Tenmile Canyon, a branch back-
forks right.   In about 100 yards, another fork left,
then, is the rim trail.

TRAIL SUMMARY: This trail takes a practical route generally above the rim roughness, and has several short
spurs to rim overlooks and bottom accesses.   The views
here are unlike anything in the entire Labyrinth country. After passing the Midway Vehicle Access trail, and
overlook points above Trough Canyon entry and The Blade
Rock, the trail climbs the roughness of a low rock
expanse, and in about 1/2-mile, joins the main TENMILE
POINT ROAD.

TRAIL DESCRIPTION:

     In about 1-1/2 miles along the trail, a redrock
(Carmel) clump is passed.   Shortly beyond this, a rim
trail leaves left, and goes down to Texas Bob Dugway.
This is a better hiking entry for reaching Sand Canyon,
Black Eye Arch, Cowboy Cave, Freckles and Longbranch
Canyons on the opposite side of Tenmile than DRIPPING
SPRINGS as it is much closer.   Driving down this sandy
old dugway is not advised as returning is nearly impossible.
     A half-mile farther, a dim old trail goes left to a
fine overlook from Navajo rock swells.   Trail Canyon
enters on the opposite side. A 1912 Land Office section
marker is located on these rocks on the slope nearby.
This is 11-12 over 14-13, T24S, R17E.
     In a mile, and continuing west, the trail drops off
a low rock terrace, and in about 250 yards, a back-fork
left makes a bumpy but easy entry into Tenmile bottom.
Any 4-WD vehicle carefully driven will make the trip,
but it is necessary to keep left--close to the high rim,
to follow the sandy entry route.   Veering more directly
toward the canyon bottom, a sharp drop-off may be
reached first, but it is not the easier route, nor the
safer. This offers a quicker way into the lower half of
TENMILE BOTTOM, but quicksand hazards exist in wetter

times--especially upstream. The main rim trail rambles along over sand and reaches an area of rocky flats. The "Blade" peninsula is to the left. Trough Canyon's entry on the opposite side can be seen. A climb down into the wash bottom from the blade could be done by expert rock hikers. Continuing, the trail begins a rocky climb-out, then gets into blow sand pits. Shortly, it runs into the main TENMILE POINT ROAD, which curves in from the right.

NOTES:
    Generally, this route provides a close-up view of Tenmile. The beautiful Navajo rock-dome country with its great mini-canyon hikes are most accessible from this side, even though they are on the opposite side. Texas Bob dugway and the Midway Vehicle Access are the nearest accesses, the first by hiking only, and the latter by hiking or vehicle--if the canyon is dry.

The "Sea of Rock Domes" seen from west rim hiking access

Foot trail into Tenmile Canyon near Trail Canyon mouth

The "Sea of Rock Domes," middle Tenmile Canyon east rim

TRAIL NAME: T E N M I L E   B O T T O M

MAPS: Crescent Junction and The Knoll quadrangles.

TYPE: Spur, but does have a lower access point.

MILEAGE: 16, to Green River junction.

TIME: 2 hours, minimum, each way. See summary.

DIFFICULTY: Mostly easy, but possibility of quicksand
in bends. Travel with four-wheeled vehicles not advisable until streambed is very dry. Motorcycles and ATV's
may fare better in wetter times, but they, too, could
have problems.

ACCESS: Travel downstream begins where DRIPPING SPRINGS
ROAD crosses the streambed.

TRAIL SUMMARY: This canyon-bottom trail provides visits
to many interesting side canyons which reach top country
on the east rim by hiking. Several easy rim climb-outs
are possible on either side, by foot trail. Others may
be found that are much more difficult. The Midway
Vehicle Access about 6 miles down, provides a west rim
vehicle entry or exit.

TRAIL DESCRIPTION:

     Space does not permit a bend-by-bend account of
this interesting canyon-bottom trail. Full-sized four-
wheel-drive vehicles can run a distance (one way) of 12
miles. Motorcycles and even Dune Buggies may go farther, depending on Green River height, growth in wetter
areas and season. The complete trip to the river from
Dripping Springs is 16-1/4 miles. The last four miles
are easier travel than mid-canyon areas, once the willow
brambles just beyond the boulder-choke are navigated.
     The Navajo domes of the rim are spectacular, and
have many water canyons such as Freckles, Longbranch,
Trough, and Cow Canyon entering Tenmile Bottom. These
beautiful mini-canyons are wonderful hiking routes
through the rock domes.
     The canyon deepens about halfway down, and Kayenta
and Wingate begin to show. The canyon bed has developed
deeply entrenched meanders in these layers, while the
Navajo is eroded farther away from the inner gorge.
This is a veritable wonderland, and the more it is
explored, the more interesting it becomes. Indian gran-
aries, arches, cowboy caves, spring seeps and spectacular side canyon hikes await the visitor.
     All of Tenmile's side canyons enter the east rim.
The west rim has none. Conversely, no road enters the
bottom from the east rim below Dripping Springs, although it has more roads serving the side canyon hiking

accesses.   The west rim has two road accesses into   the
bottom.   These are: (1) The Midway Vehicle Access, and
(2) the so-called "Texas Bob Dugway."   The latter is not
recommended nowadays for vehicles.   One could surely get
down it,   but return is extremely doubtful.   It is about
3 miles downstream at a long and beautiful park   area
below the rock-dome country opposite.   Hikers will find
this to be the best of all accesses--both for vehicle
travel to the rim,   and shortest hiking distances   into
most of the interesting canyons opposite.   The Midway
Vehicle Access is the nearest to Trough Canyon   mouth,
which is about 6 miles downstream,   and considered to be
the greatest of all the Tenmile country side canyon
hikes.   These side canyons and their rim accesses will
be further mentioned under the OIL WELL ROAD article.

NOTES:
     Travel is not easy and routine in Tenmile Canyon
bottom.   It should never be attempted during or soon
after rains.   It is not dry enough for four-wheelers
until the summer months,   if then.   Several small herds
of cattle will be seen along the way.   The Indian granary is about one mile prior to extent of 4-WD vehicle
travel.   Artifacts and geological finds should be re-
ported but not disturbed.

Black Eye Arch, Sand Canyon, east rim, Tenmile Canyon
Easily hiked from Texas Bob Dugway on west rim

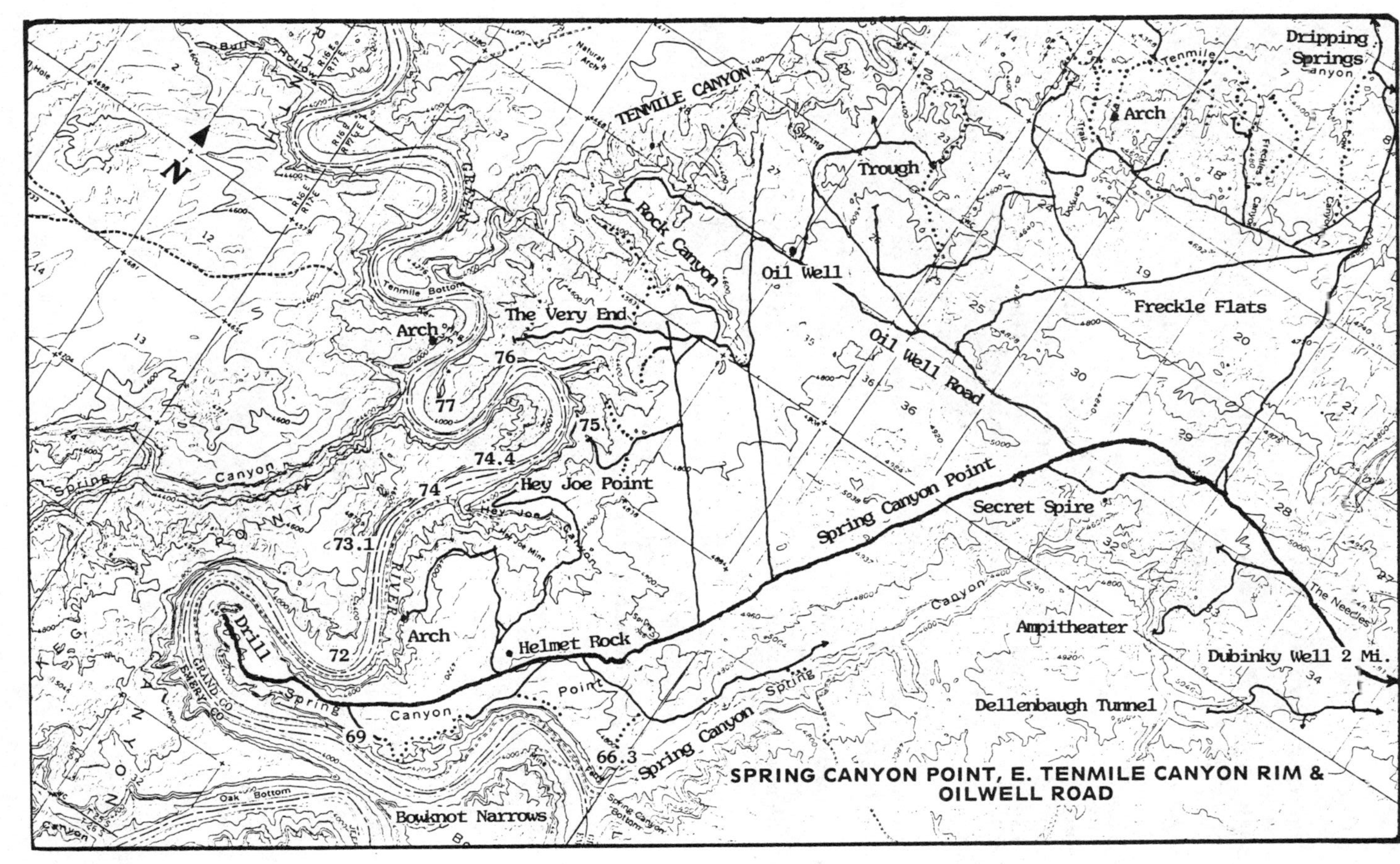

N
SPRING CANYON POINT, E. TENMILE CANYON RIM & OILWELL ROAD
Dripping Springs Canyon
TENMILE CANYON
Natural Arch
Trough
Arch
Oil Well
Oil Well Road
Freckle Flats
Rock Canyon
The Very End
Arch
Spring Canyon Point
Secret Spire
Hey Joe Point
Hey Joe Canyon
Hey Joe Mine
Ampitheater
Dellenbaugh Tunnel
Dubinky Well 2 Mi.
The Needles
Drill
Arch
Helmet Rock
Spring Canyon
Spring Canyon Spring
Spring Canyon Point
Spring Canyon Bottom
Bowknot Narrows
Oak Bottom
GRAND CO.
EMERY CO.
RIVER
POINT
Canyon
Spring
66.3
69
72
73.1
74
74.4
75
76
77
R16E R17E
31

TRAIL NAME: S P R I N G   C A N Y O N   P O I N T

TYPE: Spur, with many sub-spurs.

MAPS: The Knoll and Bowknot Bend quadrangles.

MILEAGE: About 23 miles from Utah 313 to tip.

TIME: Two hours, minimum to Point--side trips extra.

DIFFICULTY: Easy. Difficult for two-wheel-drives.

ACCESS: Turn right onto Dubinky Well Road from Utah 313
at mile marker 14. Keep right at fork 1-1/4 miles down.
Go about 6 miles and turn left 250 yards prior to reaching Dubinky windmill.

TRAIL SUMMARY: Many side attractions leave this trail.
They are described as spurs. Turns to HEY JOE AND THE
ARCHES, and the OIL WELL ROAD are separate articles.

TRAIL DESCRIPTION:

     In less than three miles after turning off DUBINKY
WELL ROAD, SPRING CANYON POINT ROAD crosses a second
cattleguard at the Needle Rocks.   At this point, a dim
trail left leads off the prominence and down into a
wash.   It skirts a sudden, deep pour-off and continues
west on the left side of the canyon to a parking place
just above Dellenbaugh Tunnel.   A hike down the rubbly
rim and through this 110-foot-long natural tunnel leads
quickly to the canyon rim.   This is a beautiful ampi-
theater-like setting.
     Returning to the main Point trail, the right fork
quickly reached is a rough trail along the mesa base.
It finally reaches the DRIPPING SPRINGS ROAD near the
crossing of Tenmile Canyon.
     Continuing main trail travel, in about a mile a
left turn drops off the prominence and heads westward.
After a rough rock dip, the trail becomes sandy. A left
turn off this leads south along a low rock mesa, and
works its way down to "The Ampitheater" rim of Spring
Canyon.   An old foot trail into the bottom can be seen
slightly upstream on the opposite rim.
     Back on the main trail, the right turn noticed in
less than a half-mile, is DRIPPING SPRINGS ROAD.   It
reaches a beautiful crossing of TENMILE BOTTOM in 6
miles.   It continues west, and furnishes access to TEN-
MILE WEST RIM TRAIL, and TENMILE POINT ROAD--all described under their own headings.   The first two miles
are now in bad condition, and side trails and detours
are used.   More information is found in the 4-WD Trailguides Publication, "Biking, Hiking and 4-Wheeling Tenmile Canyon".
     Down the main trail about two miles farther, a left

turn seen is a short loop.   About midway, on the rim of
Spring, the "The Secret Spire" can be seen. This is not
really a spire, but a very unique column.   The trail
continues to the main SPRING CANYON POINT ROAD.

About 3-1/2 miles beyond the Needle Rocks, and between the Secret Spire loop junctions, the OIL WELL ROAD
forks right. It is described under its own heading, due
to its important Labyrinth overlooks and accesses to
Tenmile Canyon rim trails.   It appears as a major fork
to the right, not very far beyond the left turn to the
Spire.   In this short stretch, Juniper Arch, Kitty-Cat
rock, and the Frog may be seen to the left.

Continuing on the Point trail, a stretch of roughness due to rain deterioration is traveled for about a
mile, then several miles of smooth sailing across the
prairies are enjoyable.   In this section, look for a
small road to the right, crossing the field and heading
north.   This connects with OIL WELL ROAD junctions to
reach three absolutely fantastic Labyrinth Canyon views.
These are described in the OIL WELL ROAD section.

The main SPRING CANYON POINT ROAD drops (rather
roughly nowadays) off the backbone prominence of Spring
Canyon Point.   In 1/4-mile, a side trail back-forks to
the left.   It goes to the rim of Spring Canyon, and a
dim trail travels upstream some distance. SPRING CANYON
BOTTOM ROAD can be seen descending the opposite rim.   A
hike above the juncture of Spring Canyon and Bowknot
Bend is easy (66.3), and the overlook is stupendous.

Along SPRING CANYON POINT ROAD again,   and in about
1/4-mile, another side trail forks left. This furnishes
enjoyable rim hikes and views along the first quarter of
bowknot bend (67).   Views downstream and into Spring's
mouth are very spectacular (66).   Also, upstream, "The
Narrows"of Bowknot Bend can be seen (68.4).   This awe-
inspiring feature of Labyrinth has been seen from the
river level many times.   It is seldom seen from the
rims.

On the main road again, and in less than 1/2 mile,
a right turn is the start of HEY JOE AND THE ARCHES
TRAIL.   This is just beyond a white domed "Helmet Rock"
on the right.   It is described under its own heading.

Nearly a mile from this, the main trail makes a
decided turn to the right, with the Green River gorge
very close ahead.   At this point, a fork left in a flat
heads east for a very short distance.   A short walk
eastward across the rocky rim affords a gigantic, almost
unbelievable view down on "two" rivers--separated only
by a low "levee" of Chinle rubble.   The awesome sight
below is the Narrows of Bowknot Bend (68.4).   This is
the high point of all Labyrinth Canyon viewing.

The westward bend of the main trail is the "ankle"
of the point, and the trail goes directly to the "toe"
of Spring Point (70.8).   This beautiful gorge can be
viewed along the Spring Canyon Point rims from mile 69
to mile 72.

One of many petrified logs in Navajo layer; Tenmile rim

The Secret Spire on north rim of upper Spring Canyon

TRAIL NAME: O I L   W E L L   R O A D

TYPE: Long spur with sub-spurs. Also has two connecting trails to main SPRING CANYON POINT ROAD.

MAPS: The Knoll and Bowknot Bend quadrangles.

MILEAGE: 5 miles from fork off SPRING CANYON POINT ROAD
directly to end of travel; spurs not included.

TIME: One hour each way.

DIFFICULTY: Easy, but rocky dips and sand in places.

ACCESS: A right fork off SPRING CANYON POINT ROAD about
3 1/2 miles beyond the Needles cattleguard crossing.
Two connections to SPRING CANYON POINT ROAD farther out.

TRAIL SUMMARY: Trail goes through some rough, rocky
dips and reaches the oil drill site in sandy prairie
flats. It has right forks to Trail Canyon hiking entry,
the challenging Parkway Trail, Trough Canyon hiking
entry, the Rock-Dome Country, Tenmile Petrified Forest
(yes, in the Navajo!), Freckles, Longbranch, Sand, and
Cow Canyons. The Very End, Rock Canyon and Keg Point
Bottom overlooks at the Green river gorge are all available to careful, well planned exploring trips.

TRAIL DESCRIPTION:

     In 1-1/4 miles after turning onto this trail, the
Trail Canyon spur branches right, heading northeast. In
1-1/2 miles; this spur intersects a cross-trail. A left
turn here is very sandy, but leads to an old cow trail
into TENMILE BOTTOM, in a beautiful Navajo rock-dome
setting. Other old trails continue eastward to Freckles
Canyon access and other truly beautiful hiking areas.
     A mile farther on the main trail, an old fence
crossing and a loading chute appear on the right. The
main OIL WELL ROAD continues; reaching the oil well site
in another mile. However, a spur branches right; crosses a rough gully; then becomes easy. On a gentle mesa-
top, a spur back-forks east. This is the "Parkway," a
delightful, challenging run through an old cattle-hand-
ling area, which finally climbs out and heads east to
join the Trail Canyon route previously described. Great
rock-dome hikes begin where the Parkway trail climbs out
onto mesa-top country.
     The trail continuing past the Parkway spur, drops
gently off the mesa and joins a northerly trail from the
oil well site near section marker 27/28 over 34/35.
This northerly trail rounds the escarpment then proceeds
easterly to the rim of Trough Canyon in about 2 miles,
passing near the USGS section marker; 22/23 over 27/26.

    The 1-1/4 mile hike through the canyon is easy and
one of the grandest canyon country experiences. Its entry into Tenmile is a beautiful sight. Astounding Trough
Canyon RIM hikes start here as well.
    Coming out of this area, the southerly run to the
oil well site is taken. A trail west then runs out to a
pure rock point overlooking lower Tenmile.   An Indian
granary can be seen below.   Arrowheads have been found
recently on this point.   Awesome views into Rock Canyon
on the left can be had here.   A very interesting clump
of gray rocks called "The Mercats" can be seen on the
opposite rim. This resembles the little African animals
which stand closely together on anthills, watching in
all directions.   This is not a Labyrinth Rim trail, but
it is an outstanding destination to be long-remembered.
    Only 1/2 mile beyond the oil well on this same
westerly trail, there is a dim crosstrail.   The north
trail goes to a fine, wide open view into lower Tenmile.
The south trail crosses wide country and reaches SPRING
CANYON POINT ROAD in about three miles of bumpy, un-
eventful driving.
    Two river views are available from this prairie
trail. Heading south; the trail in 3/4-mile, comes to a
deep-dip crossing of a wash at its pour-off into Rock
Canyon. This is the deepest and longest of all the side
canyons of Tenmile.   Immediately after crossing this
rocky dip, a turn west follows Rock Canyon rim.   It
veers away shortly and runs through low, sandy mesa-top
country between slickrock mounds--continuing its westward direction. It finally reaches an open, rocky viewpoint high above the Green and Tenmile's entry (76 &
77). The tip of KEG POINT is opposite. Labyrinth Canyon
in its full meaning, is displayed here.   It is breath-
taking.
    Rim hiking is at its best here.   Hikes to the best
photo points above Tenmile's lower inner gorge are easy.
Rock Canyon Point is easily reached--above the Mercats
mentioned earlier.   "The Very End" is the name someone
gave this trail. It does seem appropropriate--no one
DRIVES farther than this!
    On the return from this point, a sandy trail bran-
ching to the south will be seen.   This, too, leads to
junction with the main SPRING CANYON POINT ROAD, but a
turn west in about 1/2 mile leads up to a rock complex.
Here, the trail veers north around the higher rock, and
drops gently to a lower flat.   A short 1/4-mile hike
south gives views into the Hey Joe upper drainage area,
which has fine trails of its own. The vehicle trail
continues west and ends on a rocky point overlooking
another magnificent, typically Labyrinthine bend in the
Green (75).   This is probably the least-visited of all
rim viewpoints on the east side of the Green. Who would
have thought an old oil well road could lead to this?
    It is always a good idea to study the maps and
information thoroughly before attempting new trails.

From Hey Joe Point; a view of lower Keg Point (74.6)

Cliffhanger Bridge (73) below Hey Joe Canyon mouth (74.2)

TRAIL NAME: **H E Y   J O E   A N D   T H E   A R C H E S**

TYPE: Spur (of SPRING CANYON POINT ROAD).

MAPS: Bowknot Bend and The Knoll quadrangles.

MILEAGE: 10 miles, round trip, both sections.

TIME: 3 hours, excluding viewing and hiking.

DIFFICULTY: Mostly easy; very careful driving required in two or three places. Old side trail diversions.

ACCESS: A right turn from SPRING CANYON POINT ROAD just beyond Helmet Rock and shortly after coming off dugway into lower rim country of the point.

TRAIL SUMMARY: This trail visits Hey Joe Canyon rim at an old cable site, Labyrinth Canyon rim above Cliffhanger Bridge (73.1) and again on a narrow point (74.4 and 74.8) on the opposite rim of Hey Joe Canyon. Three bends and much river are visible. KEG POINT is opposite and Undine Bridge is visible (75.1).

TRAIL DESCRIPTION:

The trail leaves SPRING CANYON POINT ROAD below "Helmet Rock"--a turn north. This is about 1-1/2 miles beyond the second fence crossing and the rough downhill onto flatter prairie. The rock is a white dome similar to a biker's helmet. A right spur will be passed almost immediately, but this portion continues north for about 1-1/4 miles to the rim of Hey Joe Canyon. Rimrock balconies show where old cable pylons were anchored. A bit of petrified wood may be found. The dim trail turns toward the river and, upon reaching the rim (74), weaves along the dirt and rock flats, finally dropping into a slightly lower flat. Parking is soon necessary. A nice "lunch rock" will be noticed ahead as hiking begins. Left of this, and below the rim (73.1) will be seen the large, flat Cliffhanger Bridge, which is accessible by carefully hiking down. This beauty was documented in 1986. Labyrinth Canyon is rather narrow at this point.

The trail around the heads of Hey Joe begins as a right turn very soon after leaving SPRING CANYON POINT ROAD. It crosses some rough rock, enters a feeder wash, and climbs out prior to the pour-off into Hey Joe. The two heads of the canyon are rounded, and the trail proceeds west toward the river gorge (74.4). A slight prominence is then rounded, and the trail ends on a rock flat overlooking the river (74.8). Short hikes from the vehicle along the gorge rim are rewarding. The gorge is very photogenic in this area. Binoculars are a great help in getting a better look at the three-holed opening called Undine Bridges, on Keg Point opposite.

NOTES:
    This trail is not one of the easier ones to follow.
It has some short but rough slickrock crossings, and
some confusing side trails. The double heads of Hey Joe
Canyon extend to the base of the giant rock butte, "Hey
Joe Mountain." In rounding these two canyon heads, a
view westerly through Hey Joe Canyon and into the river
is gained. A study of the map will help immensely. It
is necessary to retrace this trail to reach SPRING
CANYON POINT ROAD.

Lower gorge view; Tenmile Canyon east rim

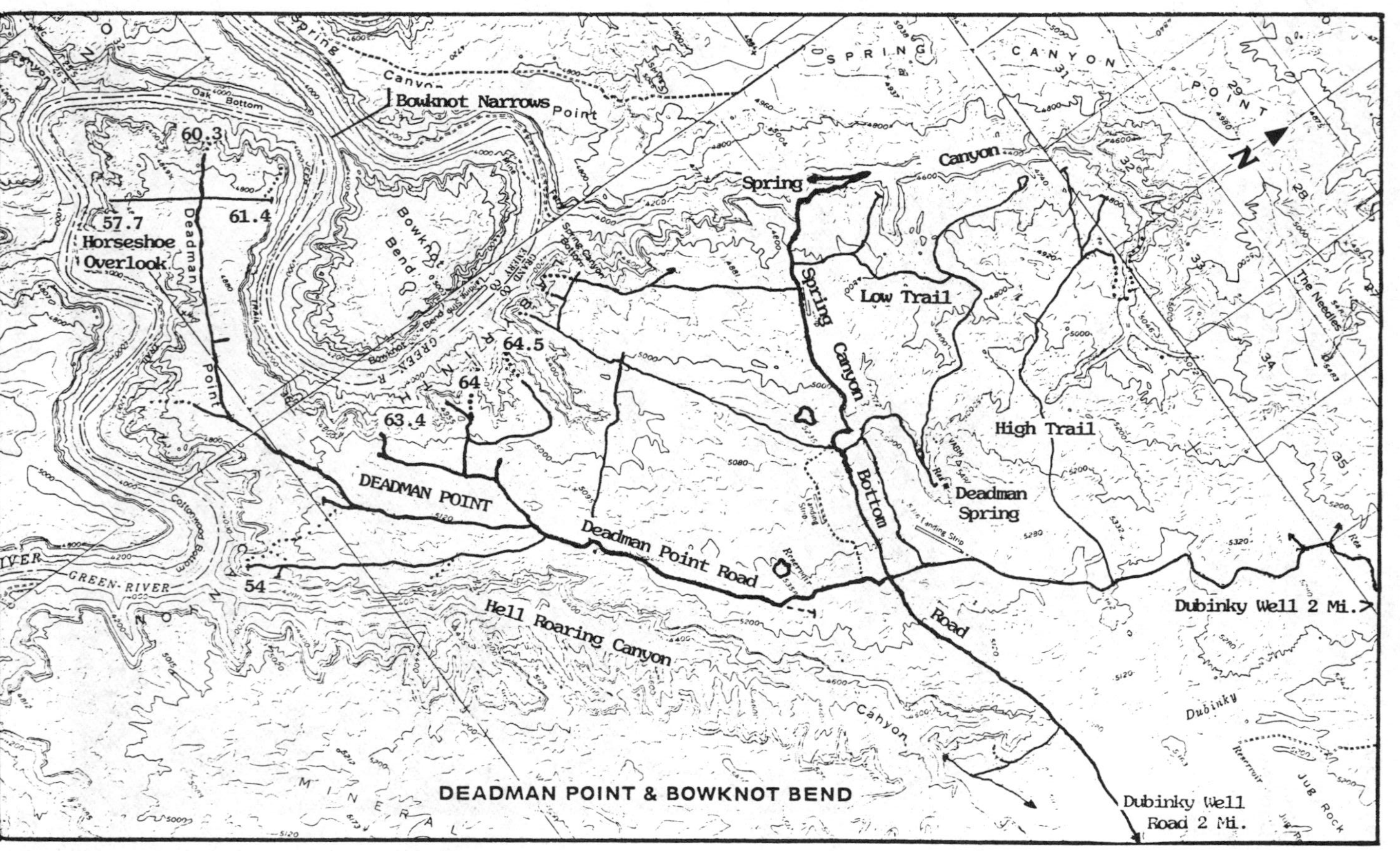
N
SPRING CANYON
POINT
The Needles
Bowknot Narrows Point
Spring
Canyon
Spring Canyon
Low Trail
High Trail
Deadman Spring
VABM
Red
Bottom
Landing Strip
Reservoir
Horseshoe Overlook
Deadman Point
DEADMAN POINT
Deadman Point Road
Road
Hell Roaring Canyon
Canyon
GREEN RIVER
Cottonwood Bottom
MINERAL
Bowknot Bend
GRAND & EMERY
GREEN R
NORTH
Oak Bottom
Dubinky Well 2 Mi.
Dubinky Well Road 2 Mi.
Dubinky
Jug Rock
Reservoir
60.3
57.7
61.4
64.5
64
63.4
54
DEADMAN POINT & BOWKNOT BEND

TRAIL NAME: **D E A D M A N   P O I N T**

TYPE: A loop trail with a long spur and many sub-spurs.

MAPS: The Knoll and Bowknot Bend quadrangles.

MILEAGE: 9.5 miles to farthest extent of Deadman, from departure of Spring Canyon Bottom Road. Loop trail about 7 miles. Spurs taken to rim are short, usually less than 1/4 mile.

TIME: All day if several overlooks are visited.

DIFFICULTY: Mostly easy for four-wheel-drive. Limited access on main trails using two-wheel-drive vehicles.

ACCESS: Via DEAD HORSE POINT ROAD, DUBINKY WELL ROAD, and SPRING CANYON BOTTOM ROAD.

TRAIL SUMMARY: Trails, loops, and sub-spurs lead to eight easily reached Labyrinth Canyon overlooks between Spring Canyon and Hell Roaring Canyon mouths, with little or no hiking.   Several good views into Hell Roaring and Spring Canyons are easily attained.

TRAIL DESCRIPTION:

Deadman Point's intricate network of interesting trails and grand Labyrinth overlooks are, for the most part, very easily reached with four-wheel-drive, and to a limited extent, even two-wheel-drive vehicles having good clearance and driven by persons accustomed to rough-country driving.   In either case, of course, conditions do change, and the driver must rely on his own good judgement at all times.

The Deadman Point area is reached by leaving the DEAD HORSE POINT ROAD (Utah 313) at DUBINKY WELL ROAD-- a right turn opposite mile marker 14.   In 1-1/4 miles, the desired Spring Canyon Bottom Road continues straight ahead. In about 4-1/2 miles, the deep dip through lower Dubinky Wash is crossed, and 2-1/2 miles beyond, DEAD- MAN POINT ROAD crosses the SPRING CANYON BOTTOM ROAD somewhat diagonally and not too noticeably.   2-1/2 miles farther beyond this Deadman access, a second road branches left into Deadman country. These two roads are the main accesses to this country. Both these roads are indicated by the presence of imposing Navajo rock clumps near their beginnings. The SPRING CANYON BOTTOM ROAD continues and reaches the dugway into Spring Canyon in about 1-1/4 miles.   A third trail into Deadman Point country turns left from SPRING CANYON BOTTOM ROAD very near its point of descent into Spring Canyon.   This could be considered an exit trail as it connects with the lower end of the second trail near the mouth of Spring Canyon.

The first, and longest, of these three accesses, reaches the farthest point of vehicular travel. A short hike, then, provides a look into Oak Bottom, a portion of Keg Point below the Bowknot Narrows(60.3).

1/2 mile prior to this Deadman trail ending, a cross-trail is seen. The right or northerly trail ends in 1/2 mile at Bowknot Bend rim (61.4), just above the Bowknot Narrows. A 1/4-mile hike westerly and upon a higher point provides views into the low saddle of the Narrows. This narrow, low stretch of Chinle is all that keeps the Green from short-cutting and discontinuing the Bowknot "Island" loop circulation.

A left (southerly) turn onto this cross-trail leads to a spectacular view directly into the mouth of the famed Horseshoe Canyon on the opposite rim. This 1/2-mile jaunt is a bit obscure in rimrock, but vehicles can reach the edge of the Labyrinth Rim, on a perch 800 feet above the Green (57.7). Below Horseshoe mouth is The Spur, and above, the grand Twomile Point. These magnificent points are also quite accessible and are described in the west side trails section.

Hikes to the rim of Hell Roaring are available along the main stretch of trail. An old four-wheel-drive trail along Hell Roaring Canyon rim reaches the last point of land between Hell Roaring Canyon and the river gorge (54). This old trail is hard to follow in a blow sand patch, but it runs unerringly to its grand destination. Vehicles can be parked 20 feet from the point's edge, for a magnificent view through the mouth of Hell Roaring and down the Green about 2-1/2 miles. The Spur rim is on the opposite side, and a great portion of the Mineral Point rim is visible downstream. This forks left off the main trail in the vicinity of the old drill sites about 4 miles down the main trail.

A fork to the right off the main Deadman Point trail in this same area, climbs a slight ridge and travels it about 1/2 mile southward. At the end of the ridge, a trail heads west (right) to the fourth quadrant rim of Bowknot Bend (62.5). This ridge spur also has reconnection with the main trail in this vicinity. Another spur just prior to this leads off the ridge (right) to an interesting point (63.4) looking across the Green to the farthest of the old uranium mine trails.

The Bowknot "Island" must have been a good uranium producer. A ferry was in service to this "island" in the late fifties and the early sixties. Ore was hauled up Spring Canyon and out at the dugway, and the SPRING CANYON BOTTOM ROAD brought it to pavement.

Returning on this latter spur, a trail forks left. This proceeds mostly north, and rounds an area of cones, spires and deep cuts not often seen in the river rims where the Wingate is prominent. This little trail curves westward and ends at a long, flat rock point that can be hiked easily out to a spectacular river overlook

(64).   An   old US General Land Office survey marker may
be   seen standing in a rock cairn about halfway out   the
point.
     At   about 2-1/3 miles into the DEADMAN   POINT   ROAD
from   the SPRING CANYON BOTTOM ROAD,   a right fork heads
west,   passing the head of a short but deep-cut   canyon.
This   is   the trail which connects the main Point   road
with   the other two access roads into the Deadman   Point
sector of Labyrinth Canyon.   An old drill hole on the
left side of the Point trail just prior to this turn, is
interesting.   It   has one of the "Derby Hats" (aluminum
caps)   over the hole,   but it blows off   at   times.   At
other times,   the airflow is reversed, and pulls tightly
on the derby.
     Heading   west   on this previously mentioned   cross-
trail,   and shortly after passing the side canyon   head,
an   intersection is reached.   This is the second access
trail.   A right turn here leads to SPRING CANYON BOTTOM
ROAD   at the second clump of Navajo   rock.   This   2-1/2
mile   section is the best entry road from SPRING   CANYON
BOTTOM ROAD for two-wheel-drives to attempt.
     A   left turn here heads for another grand   overlook
of   Bowknot Bend (64.5).   It requires a hike   of   1/10
mile,   but   puts one so nearly directly above the   river
that   pictures taken here appear to have been taken from
aircraft.   The view into the mouth of Spring Canyon from
this point is astounding.
     About 1/4-mile farther west along the trail, a fork
left   onto a rock shelf just prior to the trail's   sharp
bend to the north,   gives access to a large rock   grotto
below   which   is an excellent lunching   place.   To   the
right   of this is the last point of land between Bowknot
Bend   and   Spring Canyon's wide mouth--and,   as   may   be
expected, another absolutely spell-binding view (66).
     A turn right,   or north,   then becomes the third ac-
cess road previously mentioned,   and leads to the SPRING
CANYON BOTTOM ROAD.   Several short turns off this trail
lead   to old core drills along Spring Canyon   rim,   and
these provide wonderful canyon viewpoints.
     On   a grassy prominence,   the trail arrives at al-
ternate   routes.   One   eastward merely returns   to   the
lower   trails already done and the other,   forking left,
stays closer to the rim of Spring Canyon,   coming out to
SPRING CANYON BOTTOM ROAD a short distance prior to that
road's entry of the dugway into the canyon bottom.
     These   trails may seem confusing to   the   newcomer,
but   they are quite logical considering the general   lay
of the land,   river gorge and side canyon barriers. The
prospective   visitor   should study--and take   along--his
maps   and   information.   Deadman Point has   more   river
miles   of Labyrinth Canyon rim viewing with   closer   and
easier   access   than   any other point in   the   Labyrinth
bends.

Horseshoe Canyon mouth from Deadman Point (57.7)

The Caves; middle Tenmile Canyon near midway (west) access

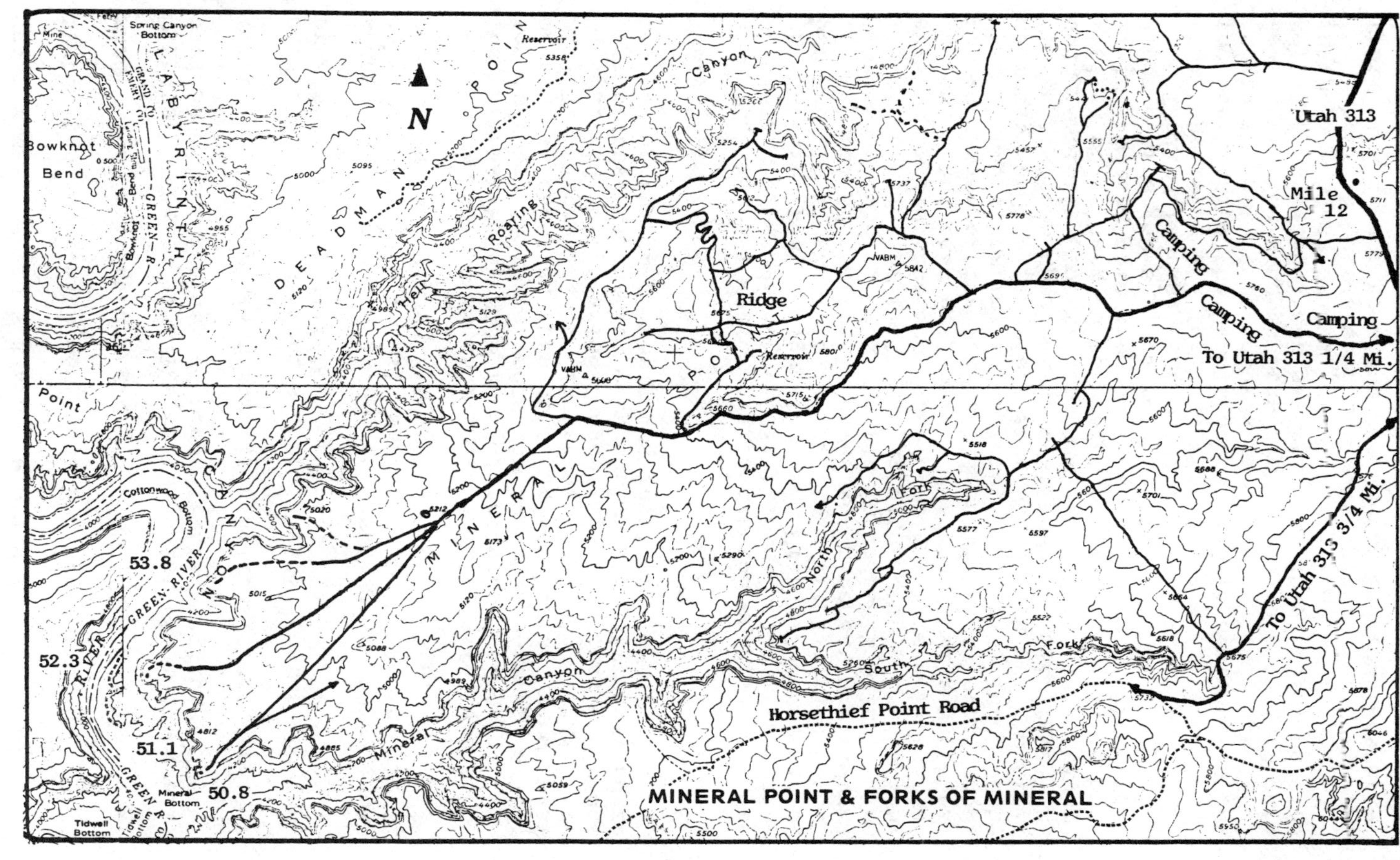

MINERAL POINT & FORKS OF MINERAL
N
Bowknot Bend
Spring Canyon Bottom
LABYRINTH
GREEN R
DEADMAN POINT
Hell Roaring Canyon
Reservoir
Canyon
Ridge
VABM
Camping
Camping
Camping
Utah 313
Mile 12
To Utah 313 1/4 Mi.
To Utah 313 3/4 Mi.
Point
Cottonwood Bottom
GREEN RIVER
NORTH
MINERAL POINT
North Fork
South Fork
Fork
Mineral Canyon
Horsethief Point Road
Mineral Bottom
Tidwell Bottom
53.8
52.3
51.1
50.8

TRAIL NAME: **M I N E R A L   P O I N T**

TYPE: Long spur with many side and cross trails.

MAPS: The Knoll quadrangle.

MILEAGE: About 11 miles to the point via main trail. Over 50 miles of side and ridge trails available.

TIME: A full day; much more if side trails are done.

DIFFICULTY: Main routes easy; ridge routes and approaches can be difficult in places.

ACCESS: A right turn from the DEAD HORSE POINT ROAD between the 11 and 10 mile markers. Going south, the 11 mile marker is reached first on State roads.

TRAIL SUMMARY: To know these trails is to love them. The MINERAL POINT ROAD runs directly to the gorge rim and is rough in three spots for two-wheel-drive. A left branch reaches an even better river bottom view near Mineral Canyon rim. There are many side trails to Mineral and Hell Roaring Canyon rims, and over the ridge prominences. These are very exciting and interesting to connect or travel to their destinations.

TRAIL DESCRIPTION:

The Mineral Point trails are too numerous to describe and give meaningful directions. The main point trail begins with a right turn off Utah 313 about midway between the 11 and 10 mile markers, just 1/4 mile before the Mineral Bottom trail leaves the pavement. It works its way to the river gorge rim in about 11 miles. The first two miles of trail are through pygmy forestation, and both sides have many fine camping spots well adapted to quick and easy pull-offs. Several trails angle off the left side of the main trail in the area beyond and, while they take time to explore, generally lead southwesterly and offer views into North Fork of Mineral. There are some upper wash crossings that will take the avid explorer to trails that lead into the seldom-visited point between the forks of Mineral. It is possible to see down the main canyon and into the Green River bottom (50.8) from this point.

Trails leaving the main trail by turning right after the first 2 miles, lead first to a forested mesa-top overlooking the double heads of Hell Roaring Canyon. Another right turn about 4 miles out, leads to Hell Roaring's sharp upper bend area, and into the "hook". Hell Roaring Window can be seen from this trail, nestled in the low blade below.

About 5 miles down the main trail, a northwest trail slashes up the ridge prominence and runs westerly.

View downstream from Hell Roaring Canyon west rim (54)

View upstream from Hell Roaring Canyon east rim (54)

Several interesting trails branch from it. One goes down the north face switchbacks for interesting Hell Roaring rim travels. A trail heading northeasterly off the ridge road, goes down to Hell Roaring rim, skirting a rugged roadless area where mountain sheep enjoy life. This is a grand backcountry hiking experience.

In the latter portion (about 3 miles) of the main trail, side trails southwesterly head for rim points of lower Mineral Canyon. One of these trails, and possibly others, crosses another westerly trail which reaches Labyrinth of the Green at the high, narrow point between Mineral mouth and the Green (51.1). This is the best overlook of MINERAL POINT. The main trail heads for the mid-portion of the point, offering spectacular views from above the airstrip and old mines (52.3).

Hiking from near the lower end of the main trail is the recommended way to see Hell Roaring's entry into the Green (53.8). Trails along lower Hell Roaring Canyon rim are too old to find and use. It is best to leave the main trail about a mile before it ends and hike northwest over a grassy ridge.

A quick look at Hell Roaring Window is available about three miles off pavement. A loop trail leaves the DEAD HORSE POINT ROAD (a right turn) at mile 13, just before a cattleguard crossing is reached. The loop returns to the highway at about midway between the 12 and 11 mile markers. It follows a fence line, and turns left into the second gate. In a short distance, a rather wide, rocky wash bottom is crossed. At this point, a small trail branches and climbs the west side of the wash rim. After a few dips and twists, it reaches the flat, slickrock edge of Hell Roaring Canyon's deep heads. Hell Roaring Window is located in the low fin between the two heads of the canyon, and can be seen from this portion of the rim. The trail proceeds and climbs the prominence between the two heads of the canyon. It goes no farther, ending in a turn-around.

In resuming travel around the loop through this country, a very wicked trail may be seen climbing westerly. This climb is extremely dangerous. It is called nowadays, "The Twenty Dollar Hill". This name comes from the fact that a superbly equipped vehicle did make it to the top and back down without mishap--costing an onlooker a Twenty Dollar Bill. That onlooker was this impoverished writer.

This loop proceeds to the highway in about a mile. Also, old trails turning away and to the right go south to the Mineral Point main trail, and west to climb to the high country rim on the opposite side of the main feeder wash. These are not easily found, but are quite fun to travel. Map study helps on these trails and their nearness to the highway makes for quick access. Many arrow chippings may be found around the head of the Hell Roaring rims, especially on the east flats a short distance away from the gorge edges.

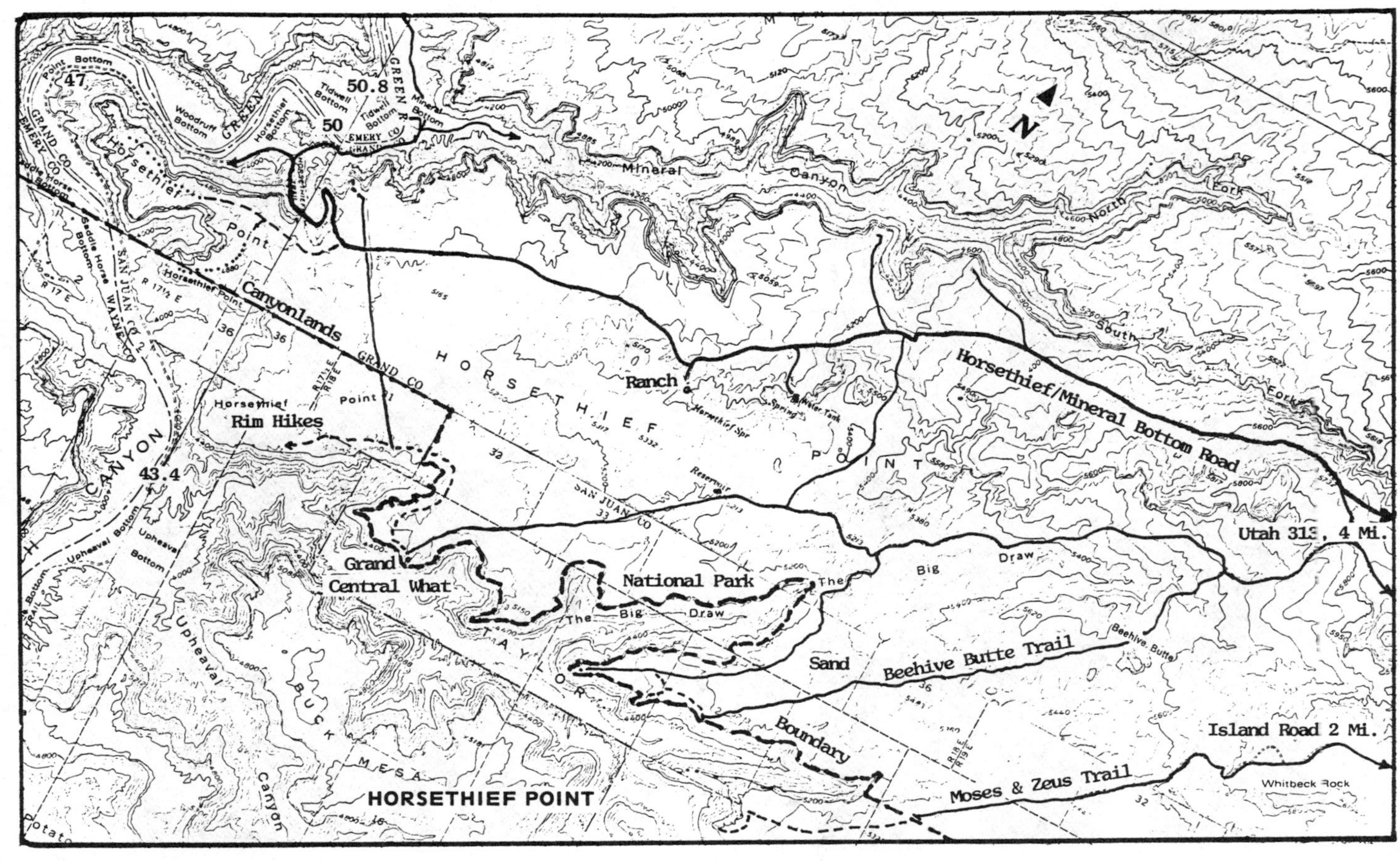

HORSETHIEF POINT
Canyonlands
Rim Hikes
Grand
Central What
National Park
The Big Draw
The Big Draw
Sand
Beehive Butte Trail
Beehive Butte
Boundary
Moses & Zeus Trail
Island Road 2 Mi.
Utah 313, 4 Mi.
Horsethief/Mineral Bottom Road
Ranch
Horsethief Spr
Reservoir
Spring
Water Tank
HORSETHIEF POINT
CANYON
Upheaval Bottom
Upheaval Bottom
BUCK MESA
TAYLOR
Canyon
Whitbeck Rock
GREEN R
Woodruff Bottom
Horsethief Bottom
Tidwell Bottom
Mineral Bottom
Saddle Horse Bottom
Mineral Canyon
North Fork
South Fork
EMERY CO
GRAND CO
SAN JUAN CO
WAYNE CO
Horsethief Point
Point 71
R 17 E
R 17½ E
R 18 E
R 18 E
R 19 E
47
50
50.8
43.4
N

Bowknot Bend Narrows (61.2) from Keg Point, by Barney Phelps

View along south side of Spring Canyon Point (69)

TRAIL NAME: **H O R S E T H I E F   P O I N T**

TYPE: For purposes of Labyrinth viewing, this is a spur. A backcountry connection exists.

MAPS: Upheaval Dome and The Knoll quadrangles.

MILEAGE: 24 miles, round trip from Utah 313.

TIME: 5 hours or more from access on Utah 313.

DIFFICULTY: Easy to all points with four-wheel-drive. Main road out point and into Bottom is two-wheel-drive.

ACCESS: Leaves the Dead Horse Point Road (right turn) just prior to the 10 mile marker.

TRAIL SUMMARY: Trail runs overland and goes down into Mineral Bottom to boat landing (50). Downriver, it continues as the White Rim Trail (85 miles) before returning to top. Labyrinth Canyon rim views are had by taking a cross-trail south to Taylor Canyon rim near its mouth (43.4), or north a 1/2 mile to views through Mineral Canyon mouth (51).   More extensive travels of Taylor Canyon rims via Beehive Butte and The Big Draw trails are interesting, but will not be detailed here.

TRAIL DESCRIPTION:

The first few miles of the road round the head of Mineral Canyon's South Fork.   Old trails leaving northward go into the country between the forks, and also cross-country into the Mineral Point trails.   Some of these are used and some are very indistinct old seismograph trails.

As travel continues, side roads are seen both ways. Two on the left are old spring and private ranch entries. One, right, provides a view into the forks country.   Near this, a dim left turn goes over the gentle hump of Horsethief Point and joins the Big Draw Trail. This continues to the lower Taylor Canyon rims, ending at a natural bridge, "Grand Central What?"

About 1/2 mile prior to the beginning of the drop into Horsethief, a cross-trail goes (right) in a short distance to the overlook of Labyrinth through Mineral Canyon's mouth (51).   A left turn onto this cross-trail goes, in less than 2 miles, to a good overlook of the Green through Taylor-Upheaval Canyon bottom country (43.4). Nearing the rim, a very small corner of Canyonlands National Park is entered.   Hikes are very enjoyable here, and can reach either the trail to Grand Central What? or around Horsethief Point rims.

The gorge widens considerably in this area as the Green begins to leave the Labyrinth section and enter the White Rim portion named Stillwater Canyon.

Bowknot ferry (64.8), 1961. Courtesy Jack West

On Deadman Point opposite Horseshoe Canyon mouth (57.7)

SECTION TWO
Access Roads -- West Rims of Labyrinth

For ease of explanation, this book describes all the west rim trails as emanating from the Green River Road with travel on same beginning at its NORTH end; Green River town. Its southerly extent is at the Moore's Cabin junction, where it joins the main road into Hans Flat Ranger Station from Utah 24. All turns to Labyrinth Canyon rims from the Green River Road, will be left turns, since the river runs east of this road.

THE GREEN RIVER ROAD
POINTS OF INTEREST AND LABYRINTH RIM TRAIL JUNCTIONS

The very interesting Green River Road leaves from downtown Green River via Long Street. At the railroad crossing, Airport Road heads south through an underpass of I-70 and begins desert travel. At 3-1/2 miles, the Green River Road forks left.

At 10-1/2 miles, Horse Bench country is reached. Pure "moon country" similar to Capitol Reef's Bentonite Hills appears. Horse Bench Reservoir dam is crossed 12 miles out.

About 20-1/2 miles out, the road gently switchbacks down from the bench. There is a straight-away trail eastward off the bench into the Dry Lakes area. It reaches a beautiful river curve in about seven miles, and about 20 feet above the river.

The San Rafael River bridge is crossed at 23-1/2 miles. Old trails head for the Green either side of the bridge. These are briefly described.

In the very red and beautiful Entrada rock complexes, at about 26 miles, the small, insignificant-looking trail bumping up the dirt bank to the left, is the start of the trail into BULL BOTTOM.

At 27-1/2 miles, an obscure left turn just beyond the Entrada rock bottoms, is the TRIN ALCOVE POINT OVERLOOK ROAD. This is described under its own heading.

At about 31 miles, a good graded road forks RIGHT. This is the road to The Flat Tops and Utah 24 at mile 137. A LEFT turn at about 32 miles is a loop off the main road and back in about five miles. In about a mile, the loop road veers right, down a long slope. Just prior to this bend, an old trail branches left and heads northeasterly. This is the JUNES BOTTOM TRAIL, a four-wheeler's delight! This thrilling trail is described in its own article.

The "square" loop road continues southeast, and another junction appears shortly. This small trail eastward is the key to the TENMILE POINT OVERLOOKS. It is shown in its entirety on the USGS Bowknot Bend map and is described in a separate article. TENMILE POINT

OVERLOOKS TRAIL has a side trail of its own that is extremely interesting. This is the WEST RIM POINT OF KEG CANYON, and is also described in that article.

At this latter junction, the loop road bends southwest. A mile or so prior to the loop's rejoining the main Green River Road, a left turn leaves the hillside and heads south for Keg Spring Canyon. This very interesting mid-canyon rim trail is called "KEG SPRING TANK TRAIL" and is described in a separate article.

The loop road rejoins the Green River Road at mile 34. Just beyond a curve, at 38-1/2 miles, the side road into the crown jewel of this entire area appears; the KEG POINT ROAD. Keg Knoll stands imposingly. HERE is where another National Park should be established for people to enjoy. Heartbeats will quicken--time after time--as these scenes unfold. This is described in an article of its own.

At about 42 miles from Green River town, the signed turn into HORSESHOE CANYON WEST RIM ACCESS appears. This isolated but equal portion of Canyonlands National Park is a national treasure. Other Horseshoe Canyon rim accesses are mentioned in THE SPUR and KEG POINT descriptions.

47-1/2 miles from town, the juncture of the main road into Hans Flat is reached at Moore's Cabin Junction. Hans Flat Ranger Station, Maze District, Canyonlands National Park, is reached in 21 miles. A left turn precisely at the Ranger Station is the beginning of the SPUR TRAIL. The point is reached in about 27 miles. It, too, is an experience of its own, and is related under its own heading.

Spectacular Trin Alcove Bend at Three Canyon (88)

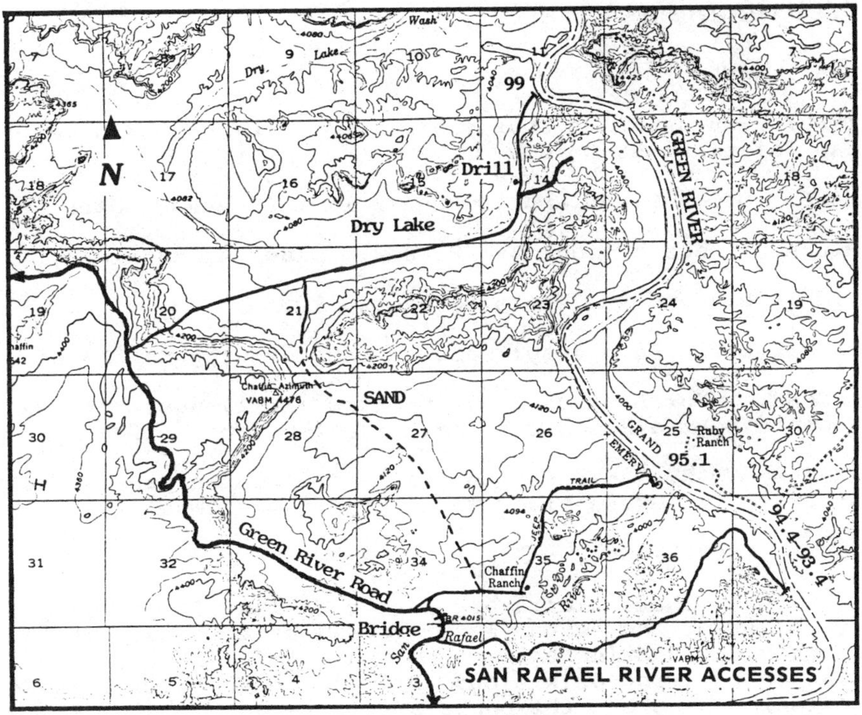

Dignity Endures ..... old Chaffin Ranch headquarters

Trail Segments - West

TRAIL NAME: S A N   R A F A E L   A C C E S S E S

TYPE: Two separate spur trails, one from either side of San Rafael River bridge.

MAPS: Green River and Bowknot Bend USGS quadrangles.

MILEAGE: North side, 2-1/2; south side, 4; each way.

TIME: One and two hours respectively.

DIFFICULTY: Both easy; some careful driving in places.

ACCESS: North side trail departs (left) above bridge. South side trail departs (left) just beyond bridge.

TRAIL SUMMARY: These two trails follow the San Rafael River to the Green River to interesting viewpoints.

TRAIL DESCRIPTION:

Both these trails are worthy of the time taken to travel them. The second Major Powell party camped at the north bank junction on September 4, 1871 (95.1), where they found arrow points and explored the area. The giant cottonwoods along the banks are remarkable. Ruby Ranch can be seen across the river. The trail passes the old Chaffin Ranch site, with its interesting historic resid- ence and ancient farming equipment lying about. An abandoned drill site spews putrid water about every 20 minutes. Utah Power and Light Company bought this and other San Rafael ranches so as to obtain water rights.

The south side trail runs the flood-flat rim, then climbs through some amazing giant gravel domes. It tops out, then turns to follow the river downstream until the Carmel rims edge it out at the river bank (94.4). This Carmel base would seem to have been an excellent place for Indians to have visited, especially in the winter.

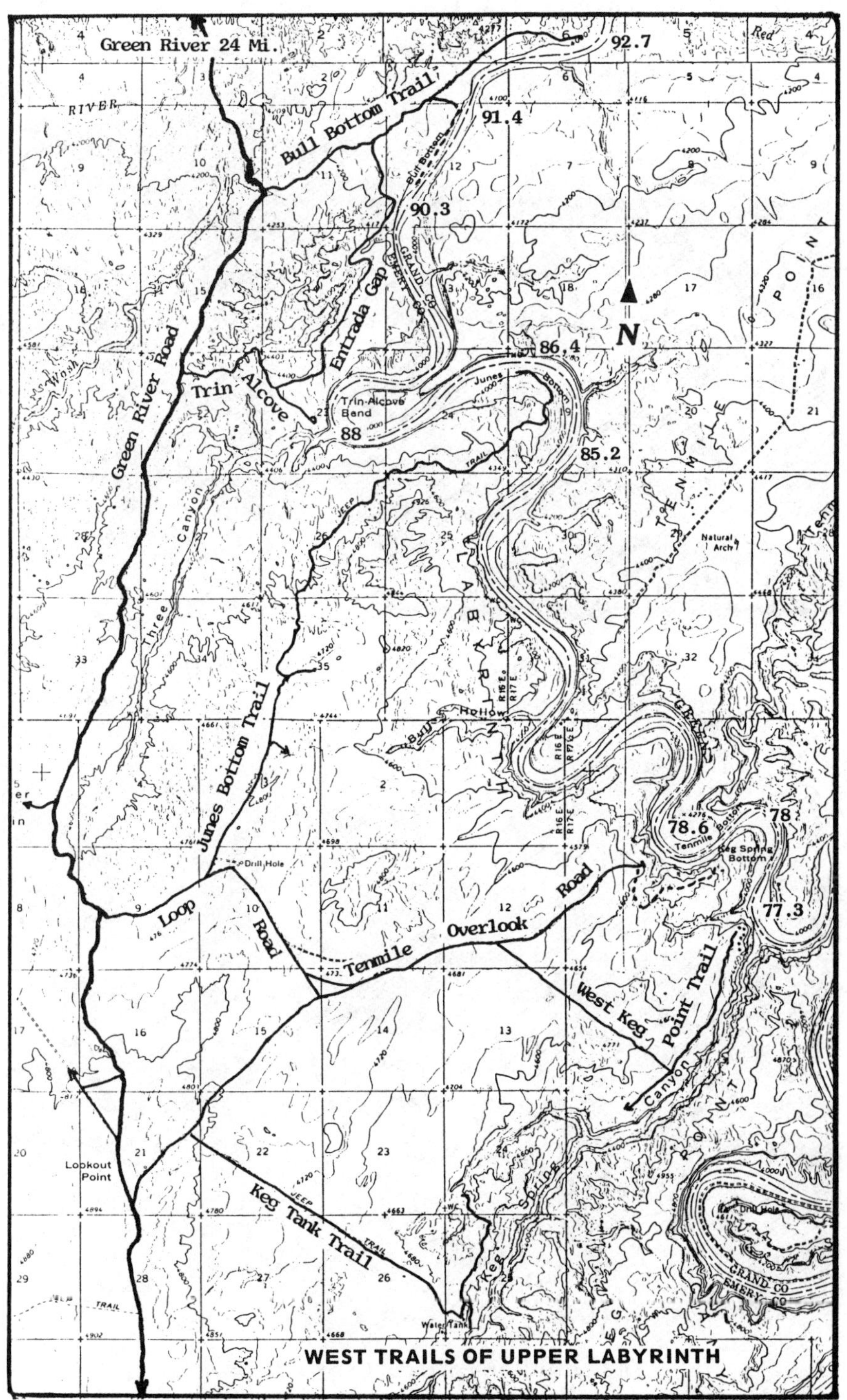

Green River 24 Mi.
RIVER
Bull Bottom Trail
92.7
91.4
90.3
Entrada Gap
Green River Road
Trin Alcove
Three Canyon
86.4
Trin-Alcove Band
88
Junes Bottom
85.2
N
TEN MILE POINT
Natural Arch
Junes Bottom Trail
Bull Hollow
78.6
Tenmile
78
Keg Spring Bottom
77.3
Drill Hole
Loop Road
Tenmile Overlook Road
West Keg Canyon
Point Trail
Keg Spring Canyon
Lookout Point
Keg Tank Trail
Water Tank
GRAND CO
EMERY CO
Drill Hole
WEST TRAILS OF UPPER LABYRINTH

The down-chute into Bull Bottom (91.4)

The beautiful Entrada Gap; west rim (90.1)

TRAIL NAME: **B U L L   B O T T O M**

TYPE: Spur trail with loop branching from mid-section.

MAPS: Bowknot Bend quadrangle.

MILEAGE: About 8 including loop to main road.

TIME: 1 hour to Bull Bottom stock trail and return;   2 more for Entrada Gap loop portion to main road.

DIFFICULTY: Mostly easy; moderate and slow in spots.

ACCESS: Leaves Green River Road about 26 miles from Green River, or 1-1/2 miles past the San Rafael Bridge.

TRAIL SUMMARY: Portion of trail is shown on USGS map. It goes to an old stock trail reaching an otherwise inaccessible bottom downstream (91.4).   An earlier fork (right) off the trail begins a loop reaching the base of a long and beautiful Entrada prominence (90.3).   It then rounds the Entrada base on Carmel and Navajo, and climbs out to join the Trin Alcove Overlooks trail (88.3).

TRAIL DESCRIPTION:

Bull Bottom trail heads northeast from an obscure left turn off the main road where a downward curve into a wash bottom has just reached its low point.   It runs about 2-1/4 miles to an old stock trail down to the bottom, but has a continuing branch of another 2 miles that reaches riverside at a dirt bank (93.3) lined with large cottonwoods.   On the opposite side, the beautiful entry of Red Wash is seen (92.7).   In this vicinity, the Labyinth rims begin their rise with the first emergence of the Navajo.   Shortly before reaching the stock trail-head, a branch leaves the Bull Bottom Trail, heading south and between the high Entrada complex and the river.   An old core-drill is seen in the rocky but gentle wash outlet from the middle of the huge Entrada complex.

Here is a beautiful, secluded camping area having short and interesting hikes into the upper drainways. The trail continues downstream, but stays at the base of the Carmel, short-cutting a large, rough Navajo gorge rim.   On the opposite side, the accessible "Gold Bottom" (89.5) is seen, and the sharp Trin Alcove Point dominates the southerly scene.   The rock climb at the end of the Entrada escarpment then connects with the Trin Al-cove trail (88.2).   It is rough and somewhat hard to find, but is not difficult if properly negotiated.

This extremely interesting Entrada loop can be omitted by returning to the Green River Road directly, but this is by far the most fun to find, drive and photograph.   Various cherts are plentiful here.

Tenmile Canyon mouth seen from Keg Canyon west rim (78.7)

Tenmile Point seen from Keg Canyon west rim (79.5)

TRAIL NAME: **T R I N   A L C O V E   O V E R L O O K S**

TYPE: A spur, can connect with Bull Bottom Trail.

MAPS: Bowknot Bend.

MILEAGE: About 4, round trip without side trips.

Time: One hour, plus viewing and rock-hounding time.

DIFFICULTY: Easy.   Care along wash rims necessary.

ACCESS: Trail leaves the Green River Road at about 27-1/2 miles below Green River town, or 4 miles beyond the San Rafael River Bridge, but is rather hard to spot.   It climbs a red dirt bank soon after a weaving trek through Carmel/Entrada drainways.

TRAIL SUMMARY: An easy, short trail to wonderful views of the extremely narrow Trin Alcove Point opposite, and the Green River's course around it. Views down into Trin Alcove (Three Canyon) are easily attained.

TRAIL DESCRIPTION:

Major John Wesley Powell's namings are seemingly always appropriate. Trin(ity) Alcove (88) is the bottom of Three Canyon, which has good river access for boaters.   It flows into Labyrinth at river level, and has several beautiful grottoes not far above the mouth. Rugged, bare Navajo rock country is its setting.   The long, narrow Trin Alcove Point is directly opposite Trin Alcove's mouth.

In about 2 miles of circuitous travel around wash heads, the trail reaches an old drill site on a Navajo playa flat-top.   Short hikes can be taken down the Navajo slopes for views into the magnificent river bend, and into the Trin Alcoves of lower Three Canyon.   Trin Alcove Point dominates the scene.   This is one of the most magnificent views of Labyrinth Canyon--only 2 miles off the main road, and easily accessible.

Shortly before the trail reaches the playa flat, a dim trail forks left.   This is the other end of the Entrada rimrock trail described in the BULL BOTTOM trail article, and is an easy but pure rock down-slope without markings.   The route turns north, hugging the Carmel base to its end.   It then travels bare Navajo flats and finally rises to join the Bull Bottom Trail.

The quickest return to the Green River Road is to retrace the route back, but the adventurous and highly scenic way is by crossing the flats north to BULL BOTTOM trail.   This is not recommended for persons not accustomed to navigating by map and logic over great expanses of Navajo slickrock country.

TRAIL NAME: **J U N E S   B O T T O M**

TYPE: Long spur.

MAPS: Bowknot Bend quadrangle.

MILEAGE: 8-1/2 miles each way from Loop Road.

TIME: 3 hours out, 2 hours return.

DIFFICULTY: Moderate to difficult. Many eroded dirt hills, bumpy Navajo flats and abrupt down-grades. The trail is hard to find off the lower point.

ACCESS: An eastward loop of about 5 miles, and called the Loop Road, leaves the Green River Road at mile 32. In 1 mile, near a drill site, Junes Bottom Trail turns left and runs a grassy ridge almost northerly. In a surprising left turn down-grade, the trail leaves the ridge. Junes Bottom Trail is shown in its entirety on the Bowknot Bend quadrangle.

SUMMARY: A rough trail with many indistinct turns and challenges in dirt climbs and washed-out gullies. Rocky turns and down-grades in final portion--some requiring walking ahead to seek trail. It reaches bottom on the south side of Trin Alcove bend (86.4). The trail off the final shelves was built up with boulders which have fallen away. The final 250 yards into the marshy thick-et is hikable if desired. The Wingate formation first appears opposite Junes Point at river mile 85.2.

TRAIL DESCRIPTION:

Junes Bottom was developed and made accessible many years ago by a "Junior" who was called "June" for short --so history has it. It is not known just when he used the area, but it is said that all accessible bottoms were occupied by settlers before the 1900's, even in the now-Canyonlands areas such as Queen Anne Bottom. By World War II, most of them were deserted.

On the first trip off the ridge, one wonders just how many steep dirt humps he will mount before reaching the Navajo rim. The bumpy rock then persists for an-other two miles, and the gorge is finally reached.

A small rock cairn indicates the way off the edge. Some built-up trail connects the next flat below. The lower rim is reached after many twists, turns and bumps. The last few feet of built-up trail into the bottom has deteriorated. There would be no purpose in risking a breakdown in this remote spot. The experience is grand, and daring bikers, hikers and four-wheelers will love this rugged but beautiful trail.

TRAIL NAME: **T E N M I L E   O V E R L O O K S**

TYPE: Spur.

MAPS: Bowknot Bend quadrangle.

MILEAGE: 2-1/2 miles off the Loop Road.

TIME: 1/2 hour each way. Allow more for viewing.

DIFFICULTY: Easy--a well-traveled prairie trail.

ACCESS: A left turn about 2-1/2 miles out the loop off the Green River Road, and only about 1-1/2 miles beyond the Junes Bottom road junction.   The loop begins at a left turn about 32 miles down the Green River Road.

TRAIL SUMMARY: Trail leaves the loop road at its sharp southwest and final bend.   The trail heads unerringly northeast to the Labyrinth Rim (79.3).   This is a gigantic view into the most extreme rough-rock country of the east side.

TRAIL DESCRIPTION:

This beautiful overlook is the easiest to reach of all Labyrinth Rim views on the west side. Tenmile Bottom is directly below and opposite. A hike of one-half mile (one way) to the right, and onto higher rock, provides a stupendous view into the mouth of Tenmile Canyon (78.6). This is the only way known for getting such a view, short of taking to the air.   Opposite and a bit downstream, the extremely rugged but accessible point called The Very End (78) is prominent and lovely.

This trail, in its entirety, is shown on the Bowknot Bend Quadrangle.   A very important spur to the right leaves this trail about a mile prior to its ending.   In less than 2 miles, this spur reaches the lower rim of Keg Spring Canyon. The canyon is deep and beautiful at this point and wild burros roam this area.

An old rim trail runs both upstream and downstream here.   Downstream, the rim trail heads for the farthest point possible for vehicles.   A magnificent view of Labyrinth Canyon, Keg Spring Canyon mouth, and the point of "The Very End" country opposite is had here (77.3).

This beautiful place is another of the spectacular Labyrinth rim points that are so easy to reach, yet seldom seen.   The rim trail along this lower stretch of Keg Spring Canyon furnishes good viewpoints of the foot of Keg Point--which is almost inaccessible in its last four miles, except to expert rock-hikers.

The spur trail to lower Keg Spring Canyon west rim is quite sandy and drain-cut in a short stretch before reaching the rim. The rim trail is very nice.

TRAIL NAME: **K E G   S P R I N G   T A N K**

TYPE: A spur.

MAPS: Bowknot Bend quadrangle.

MILEAGE: 3 miles each way from access.

TIME: Round trip,one hour. Rim trips either direction; add one hour, and more for hiking and viewing.

DIFFICULTY: Easy, except rutted going off prominence.

ACCESS: Another trail accessed from the Loop Road. This, however, is only a mile from the loop's rejoining the main Green River Road at about mile 34. It would be somewhat quicker if coming directly south on the main Green River Road, to turn left at mile 34; head east less than a mile; then turn right on the tank road.

TRAIL SUMMARY: Drops off slope into spacious flats and reaches the rim at a dry water tank in about 3 miles. Some sandy stretches, but otherwise the trail is fair. Short rim trails extend both ways. Defunct trail into bottom can be hiked by experienced rock hikers.

TRAIL DESCRIPTION:

This mostly sandy trail leads cross-country to Keg Spring Canyon just above some springs from which water was pumped up to an old truck tank and about 16 troughs. A trail was bladed to the bottom, presumably to the pump. This was a BLM project in 1962 according to its marker. It is hard to say whether this tank saw much use or not but it is not now functional. The trail down is extremely eroded and hard to find, but can be hiked if one is a good rock-hiker.

Remains of a primitive camp are seen along the rim a bit farther down. A bench of rocks and a heavy board are close to a fire ring, and many old milk, soup, and sardine cans were thrown down the rim slope.

The upstream rim trail does not continue very far, but the downstream rim trail runs about a mile to a spring seep in an upper feeder wash nearby. A rather nice specimen of burro, white with a brown slash on his shoulder, was seen in the area for the second time in two days. His early-morning braying was heard prior to that--across the canyon!

This is an area of beautiful canyon viewing. The rugged, practically inaccessible north face of lower Keg Point can be studied from this rim. Experienced long-distance rock hikers will find that to be a very interesting area to roam.

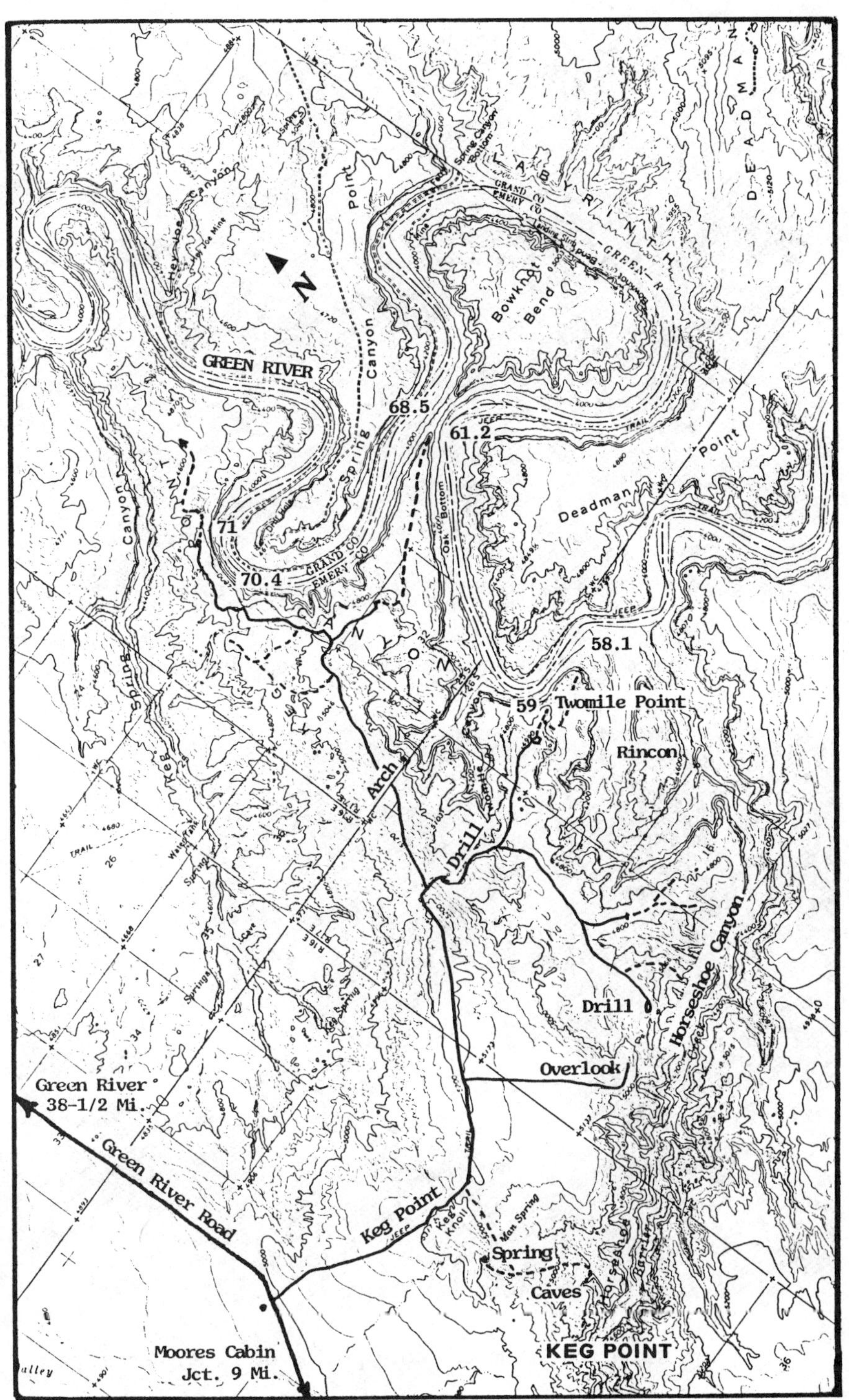
GREEN RIVER
68.5
61.2
71
70.4
58.1
59 Twomile Point
Rincon
Deadman Point
Bowknot Bend
LABYRINTH
DEADMAN
Arch
Drill
Drill
Overlook
Horseshoe Canyon
Green River
38-1/2 Mi.
Green River Road
Keg Point
Spring
Caves
KEG POINT
Moores Cabin
Jct. 9 Mi.
N

Keg Point's fabulous and unnamed five-opening arch (59.3)

A view from the interior. Both photos by F. A. Barnes

TRAIL NAME: **T H E   A M A Z I N G   K E G   P O I N T**

TYPE: Spur with sub-spurs.

MAPS: Bowknot Bend quadrangle.

MILEAGE: 4-1/2 miles to end of improved ridge road. 4-1/2 miles farther to vehicle trail's absolute ending. Branches to lower level overlooks 2 to 3 miles each.

TIME: Varies from one hour, two-wheel drive to the ridge road's end and return, to two days or longer.

DIFFICULTY: Ridge road easy, two-wheel-drive. Lower bench roads offer no real challenge except off the ridge, where careful four-wheeling is necessary. The straight-away extension of the graded ridge road is up and down rocks and sand, and calls for expertise in finding continuation in sand, and in rock climbs.

ACCESS: Turns left from GREEN RIVER ROAD at 38.5 miles.

SUMMARY: This trail offers much to the sight-seer; a natural arch of five openings, two old "residential" caves, a spring cave, three overlooks of lower Horseshoe Canyon, several of Keg Spring Canyon, four overlooks of Labyrinth Canyon, challenging four-wheel-drive trails, and superb 360-degree viewing of the interlacing points. The low Narrows of Bowknot Bend are visible.

TRAIL DESCRIPTION:

This is one of the most spectacular groups of closely-connected trails and exhilarating viewpoints of the entire Labyrinth Canyon country. With short drives emanating mostly from points along the improved road, all the above can be seen.

Just beyond Keg Knoll, a hike to the Knoll's Old Man Spring and cowboy cave is nice. Down this drainway, and into the Navajo mounds, two old "residential" caves can be found in an ampitheater recess of Horseshoe Canyon's rim. These were outlaws' "homes away from home". Their names were carved there in 1924.

About 3-1/3 miles out, a straight-away trail leads to a fine Navajo playa-top mesa overlooking Horseshoe canyon about 6 miles above the mouth.

At the end (4-1/2 miles) of the improved road, major trails extend two ways; straight-away, and down (right) roughly to the lower flats.

The 4-1/2 mile extension of the main trail is a rough one. No survey lines are on the maps here, but the quadrangle label "KEG POINT," has the "P" over the end of the trail. A short hike east to the rim (71.1),gives views of Spring Canyon Point, which were also had along the trail (70.4) in the roughest climbs of this last portion of vehicular travel. Keg Spring Canyon rim is very close by to the west. This is rough country at its roughest, with a very rough trail.

Travel from this trail ending continues only by hiking down a precariously steep slope, and completing the last four miles to the point by slow, very rough hiking. This is for "pro's".

Another hike of 2-1/2 miles for experienced rock-hikers, is from the NW corner of sec. 32, T 25 S, R 17 E, off a steep rim just below top center of this section, and eastward to the sharp point overlooking the low saddle of the Bowknot Bend Narrows (61.2 & 68.5). At only 1 mile out the straight-away rocky ridge trail, a side track may be noticed to the right. It ends quickly at a turn-around. Hiking begins here, over to the rim overlooking Twomile Canyon far below. This is not suitable for the inexperienced rock-hiker, but on this rim is located "Natural Arch". This big beauty is shown on the quadrangle map. It has two rooms, two top vents and three front openings. It is probable that only a handful of people have ever seen it, but like most of Labyrinth; it awaits dedicated visitors.

The second trail (right) from the end of the graded road becomes quite easy on the lower flats. It passes a drill site, heads east, and rounds a large Navajo rock prominence. A branch leaves northeast, then, and in less than 2 miles, reaches Twomile Point. Here, a superb view upstream of the Green (59) is had--looking directly at the low saddle of the Bowknot Narrows. Short rim hikes give views of the rincon, and more Green River gorge viewing near Horseshoe Canyon mouth (58.1). There is a hiking route down to the lower gorge rim.

From the last junction, the trail continues south and in about a mile, reaches a left fork heading for an eastward point. Grand views of lower Horseshoe, the river, the rincon, and the tip of The Spur can be had. A hike much farther out toward Horseshoe is possible.

The main lower flats trail continues southward, and in about a mile, it ends at a drill site of 1965. This pygmy-forested grotto is under the high Navajo playa-top mesa previously described.

Return to the improved KEG POINT road to exit.

NOTES: The 4-1/2 mile straight-away trail calls for expert driving and map/terrain study, two or more capable vehicles and plenty of time. This is too far out to suffer a breakdown. The remainder is routine, careful and sensible driving.

Good overnight camping places are numerous. Visitors to "Natural Arch" will find early morning sunlight is an advantage to photography. Approach to the arch is by hiking over successively lower slickrock humps to an abysmal canyon edge. Not everyone will feel capable of this type of rock-hiking.

HORSESHOE CANYON WEST RIM ACCESS

The middle portion of Horseshoe Canyon, where the Great Gallery of Indian rock art is located, comprises an isolated portion of the Maze District of Canyonlands National Park and has full National Park status. Since it lies in the midst of the west rim accesses to Labyrinth Canyon, and is considered a National treasure; it would be remiss not to include it here.

The west rim access to Horseshoe Canyon is the easiest to reach of the three trailheads into the bottom. In good weather, two-wheel-drive vehicles reach the junction which is 42-1/2 miles from Green River town. This junction is about 5-1/2 miles north of the Moores Cabin junction on the main Hans Flat Road. A rutted 1-3/4 mile trail then leads eastward to the rim. It is a 1-1/2 mile hike into the bottom, and 1-1/2 miles upstream, then, to the Great Gallery containing hundreds of pictographs and petroglyphs. The two eastern accesses are included in The Spur Trail article.

Timing the visit to this trailhead is important, due to the 6 miles (total) of tough hiking involved. It is best to hike out of the canyon very early in the morning, therefore, one should be prepared to camp overnight in the bottom during the warm months. Park Service brochures can be obtained beforehand at Hans Flat Ranger Station, or in Moab at Park Headquarters.

On Keg Point opposite Spring Canyon Point (70.6)

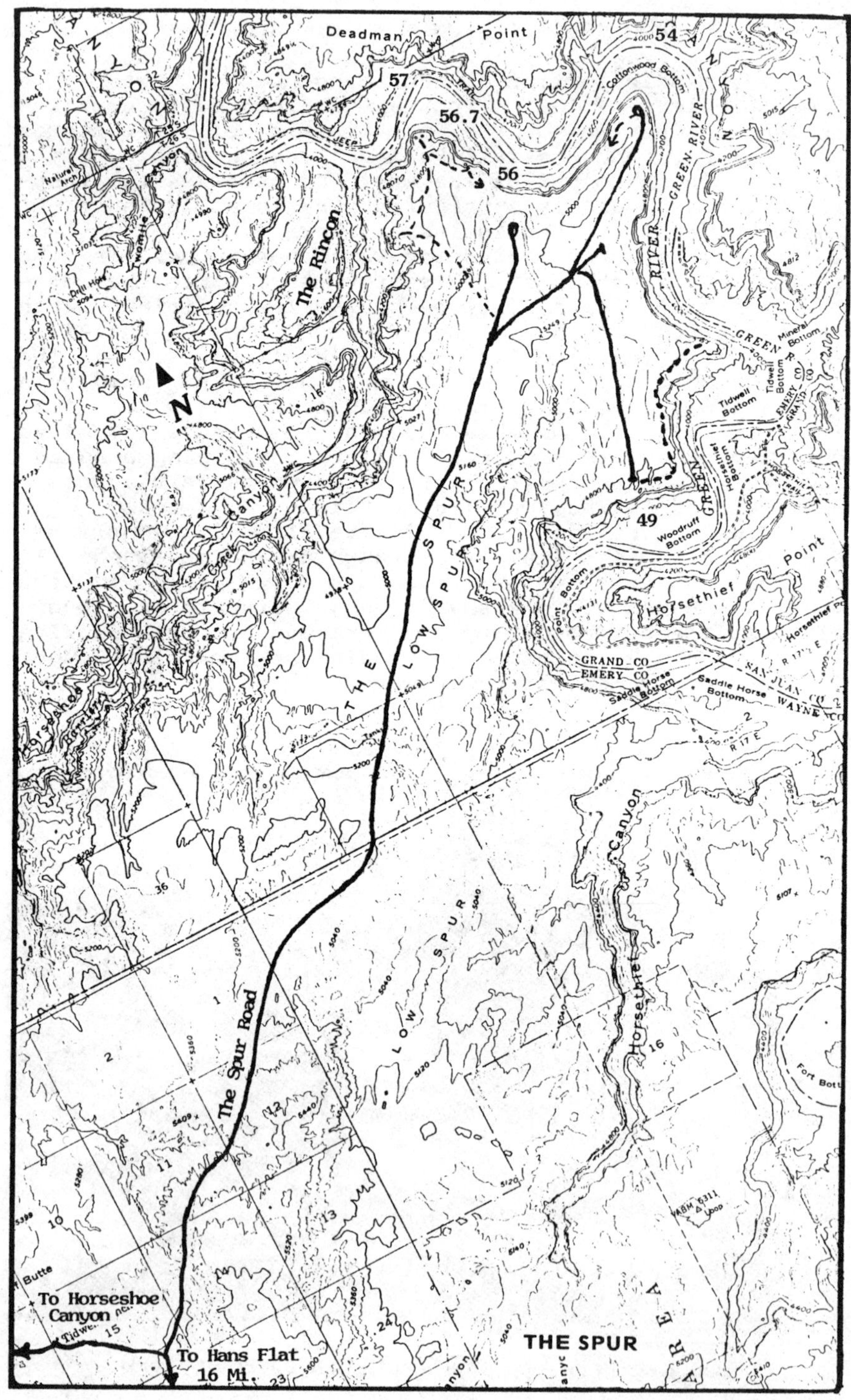

Deadman Point
54
57
56.7
56
Cottonwood Bottom
The Rincon
GREEN RIVER
GREEN RIVER CANYON
Natural Arch
Twomile Canyon
Mineral Bottom
Tidwell Bottom
EMERY CO
GRAND CO
N
Horsethief Bottom
Woodruff Bottom
49
THE LOW SPUR
Point Bottom
Horsethief Point
Horseshoe Canyon
Spring Canyon Creek
GRAND CO
EMERY CO
Saddle Horse Bottom
Saddle Horse Bottom
SAN JUAN CO
WAYNE CO
R 17 E
Horsethief Point
R 17 E
LOW SPUR
Horsethief Canyon
16
Fort Bott
The Spur Road
VABM 5311
THE SPUR AREA
To Horseshoe
Canyon
Tidwell
To Hans Flat
16 Mi.

TRAIL NAME: **T H E   S P U R**

TYPE: Spur, with side trails.

MAPS: The Spur, Bowknot Bend and The Knoll quadrangles. The need for Robbers Roost is very limited.

MILEAGE: 27 miles from Hans Flat to point. Several side trips noted, are from 2 to 4 miles off The Spur and its approach route.

TIME: 2 hours directly to the high point of The Spur.

DIFFICULTY: Easy; some side trails difficult.

ACCESS: The Spur trail begins as a left turn at Hans Flat Ranger Station. This is at the end of a 46-mile road heading east from mile 137, Utah 24. The Green River Road joins this road at Moores Cabin Junction, about 20-1/2 miles prior to its reaching the Ranger Station.

TRAIL SUMMARY: Side trails into the upper drainages of Horseshoe Canyon are passed. The Deadman Hiking Trail into the Great Gallery, and the main east rim access into Horseshoe are also passed. The road becomes much smoother then, and in about 12 miles the point is reached. Trails and hikes off The Spur point to Labyrinth rims reach absolutely wonderful viewpoints.

TRAIL DESCRIPTION:

Hans Flat Ranger Station consists of an old pink trailer with a nice flag pole and some travel signs. Austere is the word out here. The personnel are very helpful and the District Ranger in charge is one of the best. Signing in for a backcountry camping permit is necessary.

About 12 miles down The Spur road, a left turn goes about five miles to the Deadman Trail, a 2-mile hiking trail down Horseshoe Canyon wall just upstream from the Great Gallery.

In about 14 miles, Spur travel is in open country, the Glen Canyon National Recreation Area boundary having been passed. In about 2 more miles, the turn into the east vehicular access of Horseshoe Canyon is reached. This spur is very rough to the rim (about 4 miles), and even rougher going down the narrow, choppy dugway. Hikers often go upstream to the Great Gallery from the top of the dugway rather than drive down. Horseshoe Canyon information is available in Moab, or at the Hans Flat Ranger Station.

The main Spur road continues straight-away from this junction, and is in much better condition. It is mostly straight, with a few long, gentle drops along the way. At the turn-around on the point, a magnificent panoramic view of the Green River (56.7) and a great portion of Deadman Point is had.   This is a good wide-open camping spot.

In the high grass typical of The Spur, and one mile back, there is a right fork heading northeast off the high prominence, and down to inner gorge level.   It branches two ways.   One heads northeast to overlook the mouth of Hell Roaring Canyon and Deadman Point opposite (54).   The right fork of this lower point trail curves southward.   It ends above Woodruff Bottom (49) and gives magnificent views into Horsethief Bottom, Mineral Bottom trail, and Horsethief Point.

A memorable hike (round-trip, 5 miles) can be taken from the high point's road ending to the rim of Horseshoe Canyon mouth (57.7), for a grand view of Labyrinth, the old rincon and isle, and the accessible overlooks of Deadman Point across the Green.   This hike can also start from the lower point trail and walk the river rim (56) to Horseshoe Canyon junction.

NOTES: This is too far out for one-vehicle travel, even though there is not much real roughness involved.   The rangers should always be advised of visitation plans. This enables them to better safeguard the public entering their domain.

There is good camping on Public Lands of the upper Horseshoe drainage, at a left turn less than a mile prior to reaching Hans Flat Ranger Station. Motor homes and trailers can reach satisfactory locations there. This is an old drill road extending into some extremely beautiful country loaded with wonderful hiking possibilities and archeological and historical interest.

Sand Canyon, home of Black Eye Arch; Tenmile Canyon rim

Tidwell Bottom and Mineral Canyon mouth from The Spur (50.8)

Bowknot Narrows (68.5); upstream side of Bowknot
Bend—an easy 4-WD trip out Spring Canyon Point

TRAIL TALK

THE BIG AIRPLANE RESCUE

Back in the summer of 1985, we came home from a rough-country trip and found that some relatives had arrived to visit. Naturally, we made plans for a four-wheeling trip the next day.

We went north out the highway and turned onto the Blue Hills Road. Things were going along fine until we got out near the turn-off to Burrito Bridge.

In the pasture near the fence gate, a small aircraft had landed. Two persons were examining the propeller. Since there had been some incidents of illicit drug landings out in the desert, we continued driving but watched for a sign that they needed help.

Sure enough, they did. A trim, neatly-dressed lady ran toward the fence waving to us. We turned and drove into the pasture. For some unknown reason, the man piloting had decided to land in the road, although the Grand County Airport was only about four miles north. He realized at the last second that the road was too rough, so he veered away. He snagged the top strand of barbed wire and wound about 80 feet of it behind the propeller. This damaged the fibreglass cowling of the plane to some extent.

It so happened that this cousin of ours had done some flying himself, and was well acquainted with this type plane. Neither of us, however, was very well acquainted with barbed wire removals, especially from airplane propeller hubs. Barehanded, we finally unwound it. The coil of wire may still be hanging over a fence post near the gate.

We got the plane through the gate by hacking off the excess post top on one side. The dip at the roadside was very tricky to maneuver, but we pulled the plane out onto the road. The pilot revved up the engine and blasted off in a big cloud of dust. We watched them take off, then wound up our Snatch'em Strap.

We never heard from them again. We still do not know why they even thought of landing there. Cousin Willy said he really had no idea what a "Jeep trip" out here might amount to. I said I didn't either—we always find something "new".

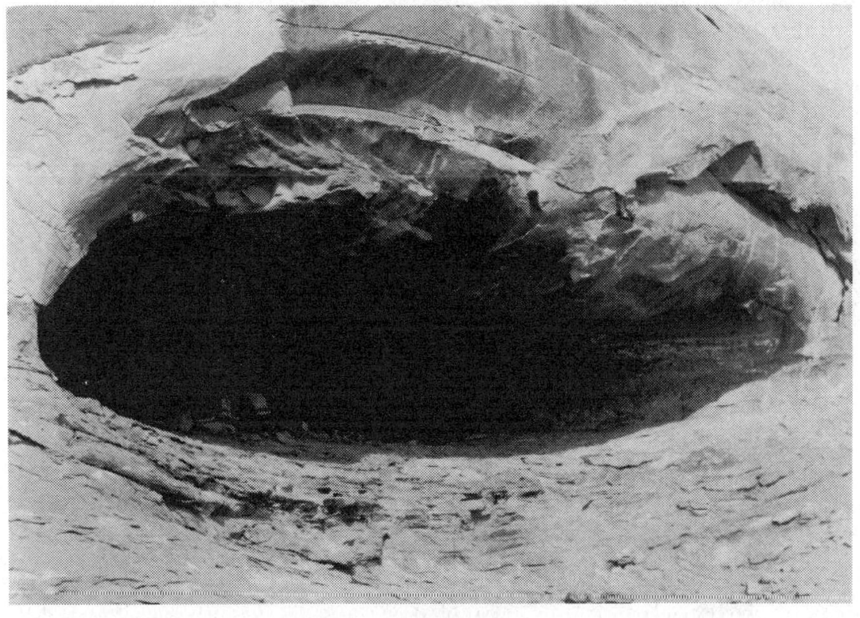

Trough Canyon; a superb hiking route into Tenmile Canyon

Bill Tibbett's (r.i.p.) "residential" cave of 1924; south
of Keg Knoll on Horseshoe Canyon north rim mid-section

THE DISCOVERY OF A BRIDGE AND A ROUTE

About five years ago, Ber Knight and I were out looking for a way to connect with the 3-D Trail on the mesa top from the Blue Hills Road. It was easy to see that a fine dugway led up to the first bench and beyond, but once the trail crossed a wide, rocky wash flat, we could not find its continuance even though the contours were easy and the route logical.

When we had about given up, and were hiking back to our vehicles, Ber said, "Jack, I'm walking over a nice natural bridge." It really was—no two ways about it. It could be driven over. It had gentle folds on its top, and spanned the gulch just prior to its pour-off into low country. It became "Burrito Bridge" for its appearance and its finder.

Three years later, Barney, Jean and I were out on this mesa top looking for the way again, but this time down from the top. We got to a critical rim where the old seismographic run ended. An old drill site was in a cul-de-sac below.

At this point, it looked hopeless—then got worse. Cloudy weather turned into a drenching cloudburst. We sat in our vehicles until the rain subsided. It was impossible to return the way we had come, as the trails were soaked and slick.

We put on our ponchos and began walking the rim. There it was! Some old tracks down through a break in the sharp edge. We walked it down. I recognized the wash above the Burrito Bridge. We had it made! Here was a short route with no mud. It was bumpy, but not muddy. We don't like mud. Most of the time it's dry here—very dry. Guess where the mud WAS. On the Blue Hills Road. It took an hour and a half to drive five miles, and it was as tricky as one could ever imagine.

There is a moral to this yarn. Give our dirt roads at least a full day of sunshine after a big rain before traveling them.

Easy Point; a 2-WD Labyrinth access on Deadman Point (65.5)

Upstream view from Spring Canyon mouth; east rim (64.6)

Downstream view from Spring Canyon mouth; west rim (64.8)

SOME LABYRINTH COUNTRY HIKES

TRIN ALCOVE POINT TO BOTTOM:
Some difficulty at first drop below parking. About3/4 mile.
4-WD required to destination. Very spectacular.

DEADMAN SPRINGS:
2 mile hike from Spring Canyon Bottom Road. Consult map.
Trail continues west and north to northernmost curve of upper
Spring Canyon, and is easy. 2-WD's park along Road.

TENMILE WEST RIM:
Hikes off rim and across Tenmile into Sand, Longbranch,
Freckles, Trail and Trough Canyons. Not difficult unless
certain climb-outs are attempted. 1 to 5-mile hikes are avail-
able, and absolutely spellbinding. 4-WD to rim at Texas
Bob Dugway and Midway Vehicle Access.

DUBINKY/HELL ROARING JUNCTION:
Beautiful point hiking. Old (extremely dangerous) stock trail to
bottom. 2-WD vehicles park near Dubinky wash crossing on Spring
Canyon Bottom Road. Hike left on 4-WD trail, 2 miles.

OIL WELL ROAD:
The charmer of them all—Trough Canyon! A 1-1/2 mile hike ending in Tenmile. Rim hikes as well. Easy unless dangerous
climbing is attempted. 4-WD is required to reach Trough Canyon.

HORSETHIEF POINT:
1 to 5 mile hikes along rims and to viewpoints. 2-WD's can park
at cattleguard at top of switchbacks. Point trail heads west.
Beautiful river views, easy hiking and some shade.

TRIN ALCOVE OVERLOOKS:
This astounding viewpoint is worthy of a 2-mile hike from the
Green River Road if 4-WD is not available. Easy hiking.

HELL ROARING CANYON HEADS:
Vehicle trails turning right about 1-1/2 miles out Mineral Point
Road are good hiking trails. 2-WD's park on Mineral Point Road.
East side hiking available from Utah 313; park at 12 mile sign.

KEG POINT:
2-WD for 4-1/2 miles out. A grand array of hikes are available,
including 1 mile out to the 5-hole "Natural Arch". Arch is in
edgy slickrock humps. Some rock-hiking ability is required at
arch. Hikes to Old Man Spring cave and Bill Tibbett's cave on
Horseshoe Canyon Rim are outstanding experiences.

Note: Refer to the complete articles and maps concerning these
areas for more information on trailheads. Mileages ONE way.

ACKNOWLEDGEMENTS

I want to express my thanks to the people who were helpful to me in the course of gathering material for this book, and in the compilation and publication of it. It seems to take a great amount of time to write and rewrite, and rewrite again, such a great amount of pertinent information concerning a comparatively small portion of our earth. It is not nearly as time-consuming, however, as the many explorations necessary, but that is where the pure enjoyment is found.

I am thankful for the privilege of having had Byron ("Barney") and Jean Anne Phelps with me on most of the trips into the Labyrinth rim country. These two individuals have every quality one could possibly expect in exploring companions. They appreciate this land and its creator, and never tire of visiting it. They have outfitted themselves well—both in vehicle and equipment. They can whip up a camp meal quicker and better than anyone I have ever known, and always enjoy doing so. Nights under the stars are just another enjoyment for them. They can become tired, but not quickly, and never irritable.

Anyone who has read Western writing, or studied Western pictures, knows—or knows of—Fran Barnes, and "Terby" (Mary Margaret) Barnes. If YOU aspired to write something beyond a few short items, you would no doubt appreciate such a caliber of professional help in publishing and distribution—generously and unselfishly given. Such was the Barneses' contribution, and I am very grateful for it.

I do hope those visiting this wonderful, beautiful country will enjoy it as much as my companions and I do.

Upper Spring Canyon. Foot trail entry opposite wall

SELECTED FURTHER READING

Those who wish to know more about the fascinating Labyrinth Country will find the books and maps of the Canyon Country series very informative and comprehensive. Below are listed those most pertinent to the study and enjoyment of this area, along with others the reader may find helpful. Many other publications are available for more serious studies of historical and geological backgrounds, of course.

Canyon Country "OFF ROAD VEHICLE TRAILS—Island Area" by F. A. Barnes.

Canyon Country "OFF-ROAD VEHICLE TRAIL MAP—Island Area" by F. A. Barnes.

Canyon Country "OFF-ROAD VEHICLE TRAILS—Maze Area" by Jack Bickers.

Canyon Country "OFF-ROAD VEHICLE TRAIL MAP—Maze Area" by F. A. Barnes.

"BIKING, HIKING AND 4-WHEELING TENMILE CANYON" by Jack Bickers.

Canyon Country "ARCHES AND BRIDGES" by F. A. Barnes.

"RIVER RUNNERS' GUIDE TO CANYONLANDS NATIONAL PARK AND VICINITY" by Felix E. Mutschler.

Barney and Jean Phelps photographing Old Man Spring Cave; reached by hiking into south drainage of Keg Knoll